Steps to Academic Writing

Marian Barry

CAMBRIDGE UNIVERSITY PRESS
Cambridge, New York, Melbourne, Madrid, Cape Town,
Singapore, São Paulo, Delhi, Tokyo, Mexico City

Cambridge University Press
The Edinburgh Building, Cambridge CB2 8RU, UK

www.cambridge.org
Information on this title: www.cambridge.org/9780521184977

First published 2011

Printed in the United Kingdom at the University Press, Cambridge

A catalogue record for this publication is available from the British Library

ISBN 978-0-521-18497-7 Paperback

ACKNOWLEDGEMENTS
The author and publishers acknowledge the following sources of material. While every effort
has been made, it has not always been possible to identify the sources of all the material used,
or to trace all copyright holders. If any omissions are brought to our notice we will be happy
to include the appropriate acknowledgement on reprinting.

Sources for Unit 7 – Rod Theodorou, *Animals in Danger: Blue Whale, Heinemann*, 2000 for
Table 1; *State of the Planet* poster, created for *New Scientist* by Myriad Editions for Figures
9, 12, 13 and 15; Jen Green, *World in Focus: South Africa*, Wayland, 2009 for Figure 10 and
Table 2; Rob Bowden, *Continents of the World: Asia*, Wayland, 2007 for Figure 11; United
Nations, *World Urbanization Prospects: The 2005 Revision*, 2006 for Figure 14.

Thanks are due to the following for permission to reproduce photographs.

Cover image © Beaconstox/Alamy

Age Fotostock/Photolibrary (Page 4)
Christa Stadtler/Photolibrary (Page 11)
Richard Green/Alamy (Page 22)
Bubbles Photolibrary/Alamy (Page 26)
Belinda Images/SuperStock (Page 29)
Nick Gregory/Alamy (Page 38)
UK Stock Images Ltd/Alamy (Page 41)
Colin Hawkins/Getty Images (Page 49)
Janine Wiedel Photolibrary/Alamy (Page 57)
Corbis/Photolibrary (Page 63)
James Ingram/Alamy (Page 68)
Blend Images/Alamy (Page 78)
Daniel Laflor/iStock (Page 97)
Wig Worland/Alamy (Page 102)

CONTENTS

INTRODUCTION

Steps to Academic Writing develops the language resources you already have. I am sure you have written personal letters and emails. This means you can already express yourself in an interesting way in English.

This book shows you how to develop your English for academic writing. You will practise writing academic reports and essays, analysing visual information, and writing university and job applications.

Academic writing skills involve being objective, presenting clear explanations and evaluating ideas. Your work should also sound right in an academic context, so this book focuses on achieving a suitable tone in your writing.

How is *Steps to Academic Writing* organised?

The book is divided into eight units covering different aspects of academic writing. The units are all based on interesting topics and ideas such as environmental problems or scientific research. The level of challenge increases as you progress through the book but you can work on the units in any order – you don't have to work from Unit 1 to Unit 8. However, we suggest you work through each unit from start to finish as the activities develop from model examples at the beginning of the unit to writing your own piece at the end. You will be reminded of grammar, spelling and punctuation rules and have a chance to practise them. By the end of each unit, you will feel more confident about each aspect of academic writing.

How can the book help me achieve academically?

Steps to Academic Writing has been written to prepare you for applying for an English-medium university and the academic writing you will need to do as a student.

Here are some examples:

- Unit 1 will help you learn how to write up an evaluation of a project. Being able to evaluate your work is a sign of academic maturity, and it is expected when you have reached a certain academic level.
- Unit 2 will help you practise producing a questionnaire for a survey and writing a report on a survey.
- Units 3, 4, 5 and 6 will help you develop your essay-writing skills, focusing on different kinds of essays that you might have to write at university.
- Unit 7 will develop your skills in analysing charts, graphs and tables, and increase your understanding of how you can use visual information to enhance your academic writing. There is a language bank at the end of this unit summarising some of the words and phrases you can use when you are analysing visual information.
- Unit 8 will help you develop your CV and personal statement for university entrance. You will also practise applying for a job.

What other skills will I learn?

As well as developing your writing skills, and improving your spelling, punctuation and sentence structure, you will develop strong **thinking skills**. You will see this icon in the margin (see left) where activities will develop your thinking skills.

Will this book help prepare me for English language exams?

Yes. Although it is always important to check the requirements of any exam you are taking, this book will help you develop skills that are often tested in English language exams. For example, the essay units will prepare you well for the IELTS Writing Paper, Task 2. Unit 7 will show you how to describe charts and tables, a skill you need for the IELTS Writing Paper, Task 1.

In terms of exam technique, this book will help you improve your ability to analyse what a typical question requires. If you give yourself a time limit, you can practise planning and drafting answers of the required length in a specific time, including a few minutes for proofreading. This practice will help you manage time in a real exam.

With regard to length, many of the examples of essays in the essay units are around 250–300 words. Writing of this length is long enough to demonstrate good skills, but if you need to write longer answers, the basic structure can easily be expanded. You can find some examples of longer answers in the Answer key (see below).

In particular, the confidence-building approach of the units will help you develop a calm and focused mental attitude, which is very important for success in exams.

Where can I find the Answer key?

The Answer key is included at the back of the book, but it is removeable so your teacher may have removed and stored the answer pages elsewhere. The Answer key contains answers to all the language questions and a selection of model answers to longer writing tasks.

Should I work in a group or on my own?

You do not have to work in a group but you may find it helpful. Your contribution to a group will be valuable, and problem-solving together can be very enjoyable and benefit everyone.

Groupwork can also save time when you are learning. For example, a discussion activity can be split up within a group. One half of the group can discuss the advantages of a topic, say, while the other half explores the disadvantages. Everyone's ideas can then be shared with the whole group.

Language activities can be divided up too, if your teacher agrees, so that there is less for each of you to do. For example, if an activity containing 12 vocabulary questions is shared among four friends, each person would do three questions. Afterwards, you can share your answers to all the questions, and discuss any points you are not sure about. In the end, you should all have 12 accurate answers.

Equally, you can work through the book on your own as self-study. The unit instructions have been carefully written to be as clear and straightforward as possible, so you should have no difficulty following them.

How can I use this book outside my English classes?

If you are working in a group you might want to use this book to prepare for lessons, for example thinking about a topic you are going to study in advance or checking any unusual vocabulary. You can also use this book to review work you have carried out in class. Reflecting on what you have learned and making connections with previous learning is an excellent way to consolidate your understanding.

Many activities in this book make good homework tasks too. Some activities such as the questions at the end of each unit are designed for independent work.

Finally, why not discuss some of the topics in the units with friends and family at home? It is very good to hear their viewpoints. You will also find that explaining your ideas outside class really tests your own understanding of the concepts.

Steps to Academic Writing can be used on its own but it is also suitable for use alongside any high-quality English coursebook. If you need further grammar practice, you can look at the Cambridge University Press website for specific resources that are available to improve your grammar.

Finally …

Steps to Academic Writing aims to extend and develop your existing knowledge of English so that you are ready to enter academic life. I believe you know far more than you realise. My aim in writing this book is to bring that out.

Good luck

Marian Barry

UNIT 1 Writing evaluative reports

In this unit you will practise writing reports and using self-evaluation skills. You will learn how to use an appropriate layout, tone and style for an academic audience. In Part 1, you will consider reports on science investigations, including writing about the strong and weak points of a science project. In Part 2, you will look at writing non-science-based reports.

PART 1 WRITING SCIENCE REPORTS

Activity 1   Understanding a science report

When a road accident happens, the police take statements from eyewitnesses about what they have seen. How important is it that questions about an accident are asked in a neutral way? Do you think it is possible for eyewitnesses to be influenced if the language used to question them is emotive (arouses their emotions)?

1   Alex has been investigating the influence of language on memory. The report below outlines his investigation and includes an evaluation of his research. Before you read it, complete the vocabulary matching exercise.

1	evaluate	a	what was found out
2	hypothesis/es	b	a small part of something that is representative of the whole
3	null hypothesis/es	c	to judge the value or worth of something
4	procedure	d	explanation for something that can be proved to be true
5	findings	e	methods used to carry out an investigation
6	closed questions	f	information that may include facts and measurements
7	data	g	questions that require a yes or no answer
8	outcomes	h	explanation for something that can be proved to be not true
9	sample	i	words which affect people's emotions
10	emotive language	j	final results

2   Now read Alex's report. Notice the headings, which follow the format often used in scientific reports.

Evaluative Report on the Influence of Language on Memory

1 Aim
The aim of the study was to investigate the influence of language on memory.

2 Hypotheses
My hypothesis was that emotive words such as 'crashed' or 'smashed' will make eyewitnesses of a car accident give higher speed estimates of the vehicles involved.

Null Hypothesis

My null hypothesis was that language has no effect on memory.

3 Procedure

Thirty participants were selected for the investigation which was carried out on 15 January. The participants were aged 20–60 and came from a cross section of society.

Participants were shown six film clips of traffic accidents. Each film lasted five seconds. Then participants estimated the speed of the vehicles, using questionnaires.

4 Findings

It was found that the questionnaires which contained emotive language such as 'crashed' or 'smashed' resulted in higher speed estimates. When participants were given questions which used neutral words to describe the accidents, such as 'impact' or 'collision', the participants gave lower speed estimates.

5 Conclusion

My conclusions were that language has an effect on recall because emotive words such as 'crashed' or 'smashed' made eyewitnesses of a car accident give increased speed estimates. (See appendix 1 for data breakdown.)

6 Evaluation of Project

A Strengths

The strengths of the investigation were that:

- The wording of the questionnaires was effective and differentiated well between emotive and non-emotive language.
- I analysed the data accurately and the results were reliable.

B Weaknesses

The weaknesses of the investigation were that:

- For ethical and practical reasons, participants were not eyewitnesses to actual road accidents, but if participants had seen real accidents they might have given different answers. Therefore my results could not be generalised.
- An additional weakness was that the sample was not big enough.

Future Plans

If I do a similar study in future, I will use a bigger sample and observe the effect of language in real-life situations.

Activity 2 Vocabulary check

Find words or expressions in Alex's report which mean the same as the words or expressions in this list.

- the people who take part in an activity
- part of a film
- people who see an event happen in real life
- related to a larger group
- moral
- made a clear difference
- people of different types and backgrounds

Activity 3 Comprehension

Answer these questions.

1 What did Alex want to find out from his investigation?

2   What methods did he use to check his hypothesis?

3   Was his hypothesis proven or not?

4   What were the strong and weak points of his research?

Activity 4   Assessing a report

1   Think about these questions.

- How far do you think people are influenced by emotive language? Consider how doctors or dentists use language to get cooperation from patients.

- Alex identified weak points but also strengths. How easy is it to be objective about your work in this way?

- What are the benefits of self-evaluating your own project work?

- Some people feel uncomfortable evaluating their own work. Is this because they feel any weaknesses are an admission of personal incompetence? Or do they feel that recognising a strength is inappropriate self-praise?

2   Look at Alex's report again and answer Yes or No to these points.

The report:

- has a title
- has a clear aim
- is clearly organised with headings and numbered points
- only contains relevant information
- has a reasonably formal style
- includes suitable vocabulary
- has correct spelling, punctuation and grammar.

Activity 5   Active or passive constructions

Traditionally, science-based investigations were always written about using the passive.
For example:

*Three grams of sodium carbonate **were weighed** using a chemical balance.*
or
*15 participants **were identified** for the control group.*

Over time, however, this strict rule has been relaxed, and you may see an active voice being used.
For example:

***I weighed** three grams of sodium carbonate using a chemical balance.*
or
***We identified** 15 participants for the control group.*

It is important to know how to use both constructions, so you can make your own choice.

The passive is formed with the object of the sentence, plus the verb *to be* in the correct tense and the past participle of the verb required.

1   Put these sentences into the passive. Be careful with irregular verbs. The first one has been done for you.

a   I used exact procedures.
Exact procedures were used.

b   I took precise measurements.
Precise _____.

c   I tested small groups.

d   I told the participants about the aims of the investigation.

e   I obtained valid results.

f   I set up the apparatus correctly.

g   I took the participants into a separate room.

h   I drew conclusions from the data.

i   I generalised the results.

j   I checked the validity of the observations.

2   **Look at Alex's report again. Some of his constructions are in the active voice e.g.** *The participants gave lower speed estimates.* **Some are in the passive e.g.** *Participants were shown six film clips of traffic accidents.* **As he is mainly describing a finished activity, the tenses are normally in the past. Use coloured pens, pencils or highlighters to identify passive constructions in his report.**

Activity 6   Self-evaluation skills

When we evaluate our own work, we often say what we will do better in the future. For example:

My sample was not big enough. If I do this investigation again, I will use a bigger sample.

Krysia has carried out some research into language development in young children. The research involved observing children playing in a park.

1   **Here are the notes she made for her self-evaluation. Write out the notes in full sentences.**

> **Strengths**
> - Park – right environment for obs. Future – use similar playground environment – children feel at ease.
>
> **Weaknesses**
> - Individual interviews – too time consuming! One hour per child! Similar investigation – interview children in pairs.

2 Here are some notes for self-evaluations. Write out the notes in full sentences.

- Experiment – Stopwatch broke down! Spare equipment available next time!
- Temperature of liquids – measured at 30 minute intervals. Too infrequent. If repeat, measure temp. every ten minutes!
- Sodium chlorate ran out halfway through. Next time check stock levels in advance.
- Observers using different methods. No reliable conclusions. Future – all observers trained in same methods.

3 Now think about your own project work. Write a few sentences identifying the weak points and say what you could do to improve in future.

Activity 7   Academic style

Highly emotive language or idioms are avoided in academic style. Neutral language is usually preferred.

Circle the most appropriate word or expression for an academic report in each group below.

1 smash up, pile-up, traffic accident, carnage on the roads
2 mugger's paradise, crime-ridden area, high-crime area, trouble hot-spot
3 adverse circumstances, ups and downs of life, tough time, sea of troubles
4 risky, dodgy, chancy, a gamble
5 villain, criminal, crook, mugger, cheat
6 inform, drop a hint, tip off, word in the ear
7 enemy, foe, no friend, backstabber
8 a tall story, a web of deceit, an unbelievable account, a load of rot
9 gang, mob, pack, crowd, throng
10 talking, gossiping, chattering, gabbling

Activity 8   Reorganising a report – working styles

 Do you think men and women have similar working styles? For example, are men happier to work alone and women happier to work with others?

Monika carried out an investigation into male and female behaviour in the library.

1 These headings and sub-headings provide a suitable format for her report. Number them in the correct order for the report.

Evaluation
   Strengths
   Weaknesses
Conclusions
Hypothesis
Findings
Aim
Procedure

2 On page 6 are some sentences from Monika's report, but they are jumbled up. First decide which heading each sentence belongs to. Then, decide on the order of the sentences.

The first sentence has been done for you:

My objective was to investigate the behaviour differences between male and female students in the library. ***Aim (1)***

Report on male and female behaviour in the library

I carried out a valid investigation and the results matched the hypothesis.
The checklist included a way of recording male and female behaviour during my observations.

I believed that females would be more likely to work together, whereas males would work alone.

My objective was to investigate the behaviour differences between male and female students in the library.

I spent six hours using a specially devised behaviour checklist to observe male and female behaviour in the university library on 10 May.

If I do another observation, I will work with a group of observers so that we can observe interaction in the Learning Resources room and the Multimedia Suite.

As I was working alone, I was only able to observe a small area of the library.

Females are more likely than males to actively seek out peer group support while studying.

The checklist and data breakdown are available in the appendix.

It was found that females were twice as likely as males to work in pairs or small groups.

Activity 9   Expressing consequence

In reports, *so* can be used to express consequence. For example:

*The case study focused on the experiences of one individual, **so** my results cannot be generalised.*

Note that in a long sentence a comma is used to separate the introductory clause from the main clause.

Write these sentences from notes. The first one has been done for you.

1   Two blood pressure readings out/87 taken/be anomalous/these readings be/ignored.

    Two blood pressure readings out of 87 taken were anomalous, so these readings were ignored.

2   The equipment/be/contaminate/be/destroy.

3   The records be/confidential/access/be/deny.

4   The statistics/be/out of date/these/not use.

5   The solution be/reheat during the experiment/results cannot be/guarantee.

6   Many participants/leave/trials early/conclusions/not/be/drawn.

7   Needle stick injuries/common among medical students/additional training/require.

Activity 10   Phrasal verbs

You may have noticed that a good knowledge of phrasal verbs increases your general fluency.

Phrasal verbs are formed from a verb + particle (often a preposition or adverb). For example:

*Recalling the incident **brought up** strong emotions.*

Note that some phrasal verbs have more than one meaning. For example:

*I was **brought up** by my aunt after my parents died.*

Some phrasal verbs are in three parts. For example:

*My biology exam was the first one I had to take, so I decided to **get on with** revising for biology before revising for my other subjects.*

Complete the sentences choosing a phrasal verb from the box.

put forward	take in	put on	run out of
set up	put up	looked into	gave up
put away	took up	broke down	went through

1 The accident victim found it difficult to _____ what the ambulance man was telling him.

2 When I checked the stock cupboard, I saw that we had _____ printer paper.

3 The college _____ the reasons why students did not use the sports facilities.

4 My projector _____ during my presentation, but despite this setback, I gained high marks for my talk.

5 The equipment for the experiment was _____ before the participants arrived.

6 After the experiment, Oscar tidied the laboratory carefully, washed up the glassware and _____ the apparatus.

7 He _____ several useful ideas in the meeting.

8 Zainab _____ her research proposal with her tutor and made a few changes to it.

9 Although they enjoyed delicious meals on holiday, no one _____ weight.

10 He felt he needed a new hobby so he _____ golf at weekends.

11 Steve took his doctor's advice and _____ smoking.

12 To help people find their way, a big location map was _____ in the reception area.

Activity 11 Useful structures for reports

Here are some examples of structures that can be used for different sections in a report.

Aim/Objective

The aim/objective was … to find out/establish/determine/calculate … the effect of caffeine on concentration/whether exercise helps maintain weight loss.

Hypothesis/Hypotheses

My hypothesis was that …

I predicted/believed/thought that …

It was predicted/believed/thought that …

… this drug would have an effect on blood sugar.

… the solution would dissolve on heating.

… a vitamin-enriched diet would raise IQ results.

My null hypothesis was that …

I predicted/believed/thought that …

It was predicted/believed/thought that …

… this drug would have no effect on blood sugar.

Procedure/Methods

(what/who/when/where)

Fifty volunteers were interviewed/selected.

I interviewed fifty volunteers between the ages of 18 and 40 in a local shopping centre.

Ball-passing skills were demonstrated.

The solution was poured into a flask using a small funnel.

Findings/Results

My findings were that …

My results were that …

I found/identified that …

…11.7% of medical students surveyed had been exposed to needle stick injuries.

It was found/shown/established/identified that …

… IQ results improved by 4.5%.

… men's spatial ability was better than women's.

… 80% of those taking part in the study found the non-smoking support groups helpful in giving up smoking.

Conclusions

My conclusions were that …

I concluded that …

It was concluded that …

… non-smoking support groups would be a practical means of motivating smokers to give up smoking.

Evaluation

The strength(s) was/were that …

The weakness(es) was/were that …

My first idea was to measure obesity by calculating participants' body mass index (BMI), **but** this produced anomalous results, **so** I calculated waist-to-hip ratios.

Overall, the investigation/experiment …

… was (un)successful.

… produced/provided (in)valid data/(in)accurate results.

Future plans

If/(When) I do a similar investigation in future, I will record all responses.

If I repeat this experiment, I will modify my procedures.

If I carry out a similar project in future, I will measure the temperature more carefully.

Activity 12   Proofreading

Before you complete a report you should always proofread it, checking it for errors. For example:

Exercise will be help weight loss.

should be

*Exercise **will help** weight loss.*

In the next report, there is *one* mistake in each complete sentence. Find the mistake and correct it. The first two have been done for you.

Investigation into the effect of exercise on maintaining weight loss

Aim

The investigation aimed to find out to what extent an exercise programme **it** helps to maintain weight loss.

Hypothesis

The hypothesis is that 45 minutes of exercise per day will **be** make a significant difference in sustaining weight loss.

Procedure

- Twenty male student volunteers were recruiting. All volunteers there followed a calorie-controlled diet for six weeks. They made 45 minutes of daily exercise.
- The volunteers they were weighed and measured weekly.
- At the end of the programme, half the volunteers (Group A) resuming a normal eating pattern. They were also on asked to do 45 minutes of exercise every day. The remaining volunteers (Group B) returned to their usual eating pattern but were them not given special instructions about exercise.
- Since three months, volunteers in Groups A and B were weighed and measured again.

Findings

- At the end of the six-week programme, the volunteers who had lost between 4 and 6 kilos. They had reduced waist measurements buy up to seven centimetres.
- After three months, none of the volunteers in Group A had put on their weight. All the volunteers which in Group B had regained up to three kilos.

Conclusion

- Following a daily Exercise programme of 45 minutes per day will help maintain weight loss.

Evaluation

Strengths

The feedback received from the volunteers showed that they:

- had been highly motivated to the programme
- would be when willing to take part in further research.

Weaknesses

- The timescale for the follow-up period it was limited to three months. I felt this was to short. I will use a more longer timescale in future.
- The sample were not representative enough. In future, I will recruit volunteers coming from a wider cross section.

Activity 13 Writing concisely

It is important to write concisely in a report so that the reader can identify the key points you are making.

Choose a word or phrase from the box to replace the words in italics.

rodents	cravings	shapes	defendant
withdrawal symptoms	habitat	bush	discrepancies
containers	amphibians	synopsis	insects

1   All the chemicals were clearly labelled in *bottles, jars, packets and boxes.*

2   Scientists kept *hamsters, rats and mice* in cages in the Animal House.

3 He found it useful to express his ideas by drawing *circles, triangles and squares* on the whiteboard.

4 *Dragonflies and wasps* do not belong to the same class of animals as *frogs and toads*.

5 Rather than telling the audience everything about her research, she gave a *brief outline of the key points*.

6 We travelled through the *undeveloped part of the country where few people live and which has little vegetation* to see the wildebeest's *natural surroundings*.

7 There were many *conflicts and differences* in the accounts of the accident given by eyewitnesses.

8 The judge ordered the jury to listen very carefully to the evidence of the *person accused of committing the crime*.

9 Is it true that you can give up smoking without experiencing *unpleasant side effects such as headaches* or *strong urges to light a cigarette*?

Activity 14   Writing your own reports

For each of the scenarios below, write a short report of your investigation, with the results and your conclusion, under appropriate headings. At the end of the report, include a short evaluation of the strengths and weaknesses of your investigation.

Write a first draft and then check it against the report checklist in Activity 4. Write at least 250 words. Then rewrite the draft making any necessary corrections.

Scenario 1

Imagine that your college is situated in large grounds with little natural shade. This is a matter of concern to you because you have been studying the effects of exposure to ultraviolet radiation.

You get permission to have temporary coverings erected, which will increase the shade in parts of the college grounds. The shaded areas could be a way of reducing students' exposure to ultraviolet radiation, if they are used.

You have permission to observe students to find out if they use the shaded areas. You keep a count of the use of the shaded areas at certain times, over a period of time.

Scenario 2

Imagine that you have carried out an investigation to find out whether group support is more effective in helping smokers give up smoking than cigarette substitutes such as nicotine gum and nicotine patches.

You organise your investigation by recruiting volunteer smokers who want to stop smoking. They are divided into two groups:

• One group receives health advice and tips on ways to manage any cravings and withdrawal symptoms. The smokers also meet regularly as a group to give each other moral support.

• The other group receives nicotine gum and patches but does not get health advice or group support.

Activity 15   Reviewing existing reports

1 **Review reports you have written for other subjects. Can you see how the reports could be improved? For example, could your headings be clearer? Would it be appropriate to add or improve an evaluation section?**

2 **Make any improvements to your reports from Activity 14 and then show what you have done to one or two friends, asking for their suggestions. Make any further improvements if you think these would be helpful.**

PART 2 WRITING NON-SCIENCE REPORTS

Activity 16 A model report

In this part of the unit, you will look at non-science-based reports.

Reports of this type will have an aim and an evaluation, but the other headings will depend on the content of the report.

1 Read the report on page 12 by Elena, a film-making student. She has been asked to write a report describing and evaluating a film-making project she took part in.

Make sure you know the meaning of:

- cinematography
- peers
- voice-overs.

2 Use this checklist to decide if it is a good report.

1 Is the report set out under headings?
2 Is the aim of the report clearly stated?
3 Is the style of the report formal enough?
4 Is there a good range of vocabulary?
5 Is the report easy to follow?
6 Has Elena only included relevant information?
7 Are there some passive forms as well as active constructions?
8 Is the grammar and spelling correct?
9 Is the evaluation sensible?
10 Is there any information about how she will work in the future?

Report on the making of the film 'Coming Home'

1 Aim

My objective was to produce a memorable four-minute film showing the joy of homecoming after a long absence.

2 Method

We worked in a team of six. The roles for film-making were allocated according to personal interest. I took the role of director; the other five were involved in sound, cinematography, acting and scripting. We all edited.

There were five scenes. Each scene was set up three times and there were five takes of each set-up.

After filming was completed, we returned to the editing suite to upload the film on to the computer. Each take was then analysed critically. On the screen I was able to identify details I had not been conscious of during filming, and make changes. It took two days of editing to achieve the standard of seamless continuity I was aiming for.

3 Evaluation

A Strengths

FILM QUALITY

The film was intense and convincing. At the Perspectives on Film seminar where it was reviewed by peers, feedback included comments such as 'atmospheric', 'forceful', 'truthful' and 'perceptive'.

PLANNING AND COLLABORATION

The team organised the project efficiently and collaborated effectively. We were clear about our roles and resolved issues of planning objectively.

TECHNICAL COMPETENCE

We handled the technical equipment competently including the IT facilities in the editing suite.

B Weaknesses

Our first idea was to use an outdoor location, but this did not convey the bleakness of the characters' inner life, so we relocated to an apartment. This led to time being wasted because the outdoor scenes were unusable. Therefore these scenes were discarded.

Originally, voice-overs were planned for the final scene, but these were inappropriate so we cut them out.

In addition, the time allowed for the editing process was insufficient and we had to reorganise the post-production schedule.

C Self-evaluation

I carried out my part in the film-making to the best of my ability. I increased my editing skills and knowledge considerably. For example, I found that editing small details of expression, body language or lighting could transform a dull image into something striking and memorable.

D Future plans

When I make a film again, I will take more time over planning and clarify in more depth the end result I am aiming for. This will save time during filming. In addition, in future I will allow more time for the editing process.

Activity 17 Comprehension

 1 Elena selects certain quotations from her peers to illustrate the success of her film. This is known as 'qualitative' evidence and is different from 'quantitative' evidence, which gives numerical information, percentages, etc. Why is 'qualitative' evidence more suitable here?

2 Why is it a good idea for Elena to identify in detail the end result she wants to achieve before she starts?

Activity 18   Vocabulary check

1 The words in the box have been taken from Elena's report. Match them to the correct definitions below.

edit	peers	memorable	objectively
allocated	voice-over	insufficient	discarded

   a   likely to be remembered

   b   assigned for a particular purpose

   c   not enough

   d   check/correct/delete parts of a text or film

   e   people in a similar situation to each other or of a similar age

   f   words spoken by an unseen person during a film

   g   thrown away

   h   without personal bias

2 Complete the gaps in these sentences using the words in the box at the beginning of this activity. Make sure you use the correct form of the word.

   a   Professionals enjoy reading articles in journals which have been written by their

         _____ .

   b   The manuscript was carefully _____ before publication.

   c   The head of the university art department _____ the work to her staff at the start of each new year.

   d   The judge listened to the courtroom evidence _____ .

   e   The composer's first symphony was _____ for its beautiful melodies.

Activity 19   Using *but* and *so*

But and *so* can be used to show how ideas evolve. For example, Elena wrote:

*Our first idea was to use an outdoor location, **but** this did not convey the bleakness of the characters' inner life, **so** we relocated to an apartment.*

*Originally, voice-overs were planned for the final scene, **but** these were inappropriate, **so** we cut them out.*

1 Write complete sentences using *but* and *so*. The first one has been done for you.

   a   My first idea/photograph spiral shapes (too limiting/photograph buildings).

       My first idea was to photograph spiral shapes, but this was too limiting, so I decided to photograph buildings.

   b   My first idea/base my musical composition on a folk song (simplistic/use a Bach chorale).

   c   Originally/a forest location/chose (light not bright enough/use/coastal area).

   d   My first idea/make the costumes in velvet and silk (expensive/use cotton and wool).

   e   My first idea/set the story in Warsaw (too much research/chose area familiar to me).

   f   Originally/aim/explore/effect of war/on/family (too wide-ranging/so focus/effect/one main character).

   g   My first idea/paint/still life/apples on kitchen table (mundane/so/paint apple trees/orchard).

   h   My first idea/use slow, romantic music/opening scene (too sad/so/chose/a lively, more upbeat soundtrack).

2 You have been working on a jewellery project. You started to work with glass but changed to wood. Write a sentence explaining why you did this, using the pattern from the first part of this activity.

Activity 20 Completing a self-evaluation

Khaled carried out a photography project in which he trained children from a poor neighbourhood to take photographs of their environment. Now he has to write his evaluation.

 1 What do you think Khaled should cover in his evaluation? Write down some ideas, for example whether the children benefited enough from his work with them.

2 Read the evaluation below and complete the gaps with words from the box.

feedback	atmospheric	advice	safely
setting	deprived	permission	self-esteem
targets	prosthetic	outcomes	scheduled
subjects	intrusive	adapt	

Evaluation

Strengths

1 Firstly, I planned the project effectively and identified clear aims and _____.

2 Communication with parents was effective and I obtained their written _____ without difficulty.

3 The children were encouraged to set personal _____ and in all cases they achieved their goals.

4 The _____ chosen for the project was a converted warehouse which was well-equipped and pleasantly furnished.

5 I coached the children successfully, demonstrated the use of the equipment competently, explained risks and dangers and made sure they worked _____.

Weaknesses

1 I started the project later than I had _____ due to sickness, which meant that the light was not as good as it would have been if I had started on time.

2 One of the children had a _____ arm and could not use the camera and so this child was not as involved at first as he could have been.

3 I did not know how to _____ the photographic techniques at first.

4 My first idea was to take pictures of the children's private home life but this was too _____, so we took outdoor scenes instead.

Future plans

• If I do a similar project in future, I will make sure I am prepared for children with special needs. If I am unsure, I will take professional _____.

• I will involve the children more in the choice of topics and avoid _____ that might be sensitive for them, such as 'Home life'.

Summing up

• I completed the project to the best of my ability. The project was successful, it engaged children from a _____ neighbourhood, increased their skills and developed their _____. They took high-quality photographs. In particular, their photographs of the market and the lake were unusual and _____.

• _____ from participants included comments such as 'brilliant' and 'better than I ever imagined'.

Activity 21   Writing your own report

You have been asked to deliver a coaching session in a specific skill to a group of children. You can choose the skill you want to teach or select one of these:

- Introducing a sporting technique such as ball-passing skills in netball, basketball or rugby, or a basic swimming stroke.
- Introducing the children to a new art or craft such as making simple jewellery or making a basic meal.
- Teaching them how to use a simple musical instrument such as drums or how to perform a simple dance.

1 Write a report, setting out the aim of the session, equipment required, methods, and what the children learned. At the end of the report, write an evaluation analysing the strengths and weaknesses of the session. Write at least 250 words.

2 When you have written a first draft, use the report checklist in Activity 4. Then rewrite the draft with any corrections or improvements.

3 Review any other reports you have written and make improvements to them.

UNIT 2 Writing reports on surveys

In this unit you will practise writing well-organised reports on surveys and producing effective questionnaires for surveys.

PART 1 WRITING ABOUT SURVEYS

Activity 1   Using a report format

 Scientists need volunteers from all sections of society to take part in research trials. Think about:

- whether people are usually happy to volunteer for scientific trials
- what scientists can do to make volunteers feel confident about volunteering.

A medical research project was carried out to investigate fitness levels in a local population. The report below was written to show how members of the public felt about being volunteers for the fitness testing research.

This is a common format for a report based on a survey:

- Aim – states the purpose of the report.
- Method – says how the information was collected.
- Findings – says what was found out.
- Conclusions – a logical summing-up based on the findings.
- Recommendations – makes suggestions for improvements.

Read the report and then answer the questions that follow it.

Report on the Participants' Experiences of the Fitness Testing Study

1 Aim

The aim of this report is to summarise:
- how acceptable the volunteers found the fitness tests
- the reasons why the volunteers participated in the research.

2 Method for Collecting Data

In May, 94 participants completed a questionnaire. *Respondents* rated the acceptability of the fitness tests on a scale of 1 (highly unacceptable) to 10 (highly acceptable). The participants' general comments on the tests were also *elicited*. Finally, they gave their views on participating in scientific research.

The survey questionnaire and a full breakdown of statistical information are contained in the *appendix*.

3 Findings

Section 1: Laboratory Tests

Participants made one four-hour visit to the laboratory to take the fitness tests.

<u>A Scan of the whole body</u>
Height, weight and body composition were measured by the scan. These tests were rated highly acceptable by 65.7% of volunteers. Over one quarter said they were moderately acceptable. An insignificant number, fewer than 10%, said the tests were unacceptable.

<u>B Rest test</u>
In this test, volunteers wore a mask that measured the amount of oxygen they breathed.
The vast majority of volunteers found this test highly acceptable. The remaining volunteers (13.4%) said this test was moderately acceptable.

<u>C Treadmill test</u>
In this test, participants walked, jogged and ran on a *treadmill* for as long as possible while maximum fitness measurements were taken. They could stop at any time.
Two out of three volunteers found this test highly acceptable. Over one quarter rated it moderately acceptable. A small minority, fewer than 5%, rated it moderately unacceptable.

<u>General comments on the laboratory tests</u>
Almost all general comments from volunteers were positive. Participants particularly mentioned the approachability of the research team. 'The staff couldn't have been more encouraging' was a typical comment. Over half the respondents had visited the laboratory before the study and said they found the visit reassuring. A small number (9%) mentioned that the laboratory tests were tiring.

Section 2: Home-based Tests
Participants were given special, lightweight equipment for fitness monitoring of the heart and hips to wear continuously at home for seven days.

<u>A Heart monitor</u>
Four-fifths of the respondents found the heart monitor highly acceptable. 12% found it moderately acceptable.

<u>B Hip monitors</u>
Nearly all volunteers found these monitors highly acceptable. An insignificant number (4%) found them moderately unacceptable.

<u>General comments on the home-based tests</u>
The majority of the participants reported that the devices were easy to use and gave them no trouble. A minority, fewer than 8%, mentioned slight skin irritation from the monitors.

Section 3: Reasons for taking part in the study
Respondents were asked to say whether their main reason for taking part in the study was to support research or to get information about their fitness. The majority of the volunteers took part to support research but a significant proportion (19%) wanted information about their own fitness.

4 Conclusions
The laboratory and home-based tests are acceptable to the majority of participants.
Most participants are motivated by the desire to contribute to research.

5 Recommendations
(i) It is recommended that the fitness tests should be continued without changes.
(ii) Volunteers should continue to be encouraged to visit the laboratories prior to the study to become familiar with a scientific environment.
(iii) It is proposed that participants rest for 30 minutes at the end of the laboratory tests.

1 What is the aim of the report? Mention two things.
2 How were the data collected?
3 Is the information in the report clear?

4   Are the statistical data easy to understand?

5   Is the report set out well with headings, numbered points and bullet points?

6   Do you think the study was ethical and fair?

7   Would you be willing to take part in a similar study? Give reasons for your answer.

Activity 2   Vocabulary check

1 Find italicised words in the report from Activity 1 similar in meaning to these words and expressions.

- asked for

- people who complete a questionnaire

- a separate part of the report which contains extra information

- an exercise machine with moving parts

2 Some words are easily confused with each other. Choose the correct word in italics in each sentence.

a   The *elderly/aged* lady refused to answer questions she thought were too *private/personal*.

b   Most of the respondents believed that they would not be able to stop volunteering, even if they suffered harmful *side effects/outcomes* during the *trial/trail*.

c   Is volunteering for medical research more socially *mindless/useful* than participating in market research about your shopping *procedures/habits*?

d   A significant *number/amount* of scientists feel that volunteers should be paid to take part in *clinical/hospital* research.

e   All the statistical data were available in the *index/appendix* at the end of the report.

f   Although the students could not be paid a *fee/price*, the department offered to pay their bus *fairs/fares*.

g   Although I felt sick after taking the tablets, I did not actually *vomit/nauseate*.

h   I got a *prescription/paper* for a *tube/sachet* of eye ointment which had to be applied once every night for a week.

Activity 3   Simplifying statistics

A report which is packed with a large number of statistics can be difficult to follow, so approximations are often used as well as percentages.

The report in Activity 1 included these approximations:

- the vast majority

- over one quarter

- the majority

- fewer than 10%

- two out of three

- nearly all

- over half

- an insignificant number

- a small number

- four-fifths

- a significant proportion

- a small minority

- most.

Match the approximations with the percentages.

Just under all	0.03%
Over one in ten	39.7%
Half	10.8%
Almost half	50.0%
Nearly two-fifths	23.9%
An insignificant proportion	17.3%
More than one in six	66.8%
Just over two-thirds	99.7%
Nearly a quarter	49.2%

Activity 4   Approximations in context

When we choose approximations, we need to be sensitive to the context. For example, 'a small minority, fewer than 10%' is an acceptable way of describing an event of little importance, such as the development of a harmless skin irritation. However, if a serious situation were being described, such as deaths from road accidents, it would be wrong to refer to 10% as being 'a small minority'.

1 Choose the best approximation in this sentence.

An insignificant number/a substantial proportion of patients, about 9%, lost their sight after undergoing an experimental treatment for eye problems.

2 Read the findings about lifestyles below and change some of the percentages to approximations. Make any other changes that are necessary.

Figures released yesterday show that young people are failing to lead active lives. Only 69.6% of children aged 7–12 take sufficient daily exercise to maintain health. The figure falls in the teenage years with 49.5% of teenagers doing enough daily exercise. For those between 20 and 30 the figure falls to 24.3%. There are fears that a sedentary lifestyle may lead to health problems. Health organisations predict that obesity rates may rise by 33.3% over the next twenty years. A health promotion campaign starting on major TV channels aims to increase the popularity of exercise and will emphasise the importance of a balanced diet.

Activity 5   Making recommendations

Reports on surveys often include recommendations for changes or improvements. The following phrases are suitable for recommendations.

It is recommended/proposed that ...

It is recommended that the tests are used on an older sector of the population.

A final recommendation is that ...

A final recommendation is that only volunteers in good health should be accepted for the study.

Note that *should* is often used to make recommendations.

*It is recommended that the laboratory measurement tests and the home measurement tests **should** be continued without changes.*

Should is suitable for most situations when making recommendations in reports.

From your work on Unit 1 you will know that passive constructions are often used in reports.

You already know that the passive voice is formed with the object of the sentence, the verb *to be* in the correct tense, and the past participle of the verb required. For example:

We recommend purchasing a new machine.

It is recommended that a new machine is purchased.

We recommend telling participants to relax while we conduct the tests.

It is recommended *that participants are told to relax while the tests are being conducted.*

We should tell volunteers not to chew gum during the tests.

Volunteers should be told *not to chew gum during the tests.*

1 **Look back at the report in Activity 1 and underline two sentences in the passive and two in active constructions.**

2 **The sentences below come from the recommendations sections of survey reports. They are in active constructions. Change them to passive constructions. Use *should* in some of the passive sentences.**

    a I propose increasing the number of participants in the study to 60.
       It is proposed …

    b I recommend telling volunteers about any physical abnormalities we detect.
       It is recommended …

    c I propose emphasising the benefits to the participants of knowing their fitness levels.
       It is proposed …

    d I recommend that volunteers rest after the exercises.
       It is …

    e I propose telling volunteers not to smoke before the tests.
       It …

    f I propose that we measure the heart rates of volunteers.

    g I recommend telling participants they can withdraw at any time we are conducting the research.

    h Finally, I recommend that we do not recruit volunteers under the age of 18.

Activity 6 Completing a report based on a survey

1 **Read the paragraph below. What problem did the research team have and what was done about it?**

A medical research team at Newlands Hospital found it difficult to recruit volunteers for their research projects. They carried out a survey to find out why. A questionnaire was completed by 500 members of the general public aged 18 to 55 years, both men and women. The results showed that while 100 people said they would participate, 400 respondents said they would refuse. The information from the survey will be used by the research team to improve the way they recruit volunteers and carry out trials.

2 **Now study the data below and answer the questions.**

Reasons for not participating in medical research	%
Would find clinical environment too strange	23.0
Worried about bad effects on health	9.0
Too busy	10.0
Would feel uncomfortable being interviewed or examined by research team	30.0
No benefit for myself	11.5

(continued)

Difficult to withdraw from a trial	5.5
Did not know opportunities existed	6.0
Other	5.0

a What were the majority of respondents worried about?

b What could be done by the research team to make people more likely to volunteer? Think of ideas in pairs and then discuss them in groups.

Activity 7   Writing a report

Write a report outlining what was found out by the survey. In your recommendations, suggest improvements which would encourage more people to volunteer. Use the report format below. Remember that bullet points and numbered points are helpful in sub-sections of a report.

Title

1 Aim

2 Method

3 Findings

4 Conclusion

5 Recommendations

Activity 8   Writing concisely

It is natural to use unnecessary words when we speak, but when we write for academic purposes we should try to be concise. For example:

All the separate and different laboratory measurements that were taken and recorded were fed into the computer program.

could be written more concisely as:

All the laboratory measurements were fed into the computer program.

Cross out the unnecessary words in these sentences without changing the meaning.

1 Participants walked continuously for twenty minutes on the treadmill, without stopping to rest for even a few moments.

2 Any volunteers under the age of 18 who applied to take part in the tests were not allowed to participate unless they had a signed parental consent form giving them permission to participate in the study.

3 All information is confidential and any information identifying individuals, and their names and addresses, is removed from the documentation so that individuals can be completely sure they will not be recognised at any point in the future.

4 A final recommendation is that volunteers are invited to the laboratory before the start of the study so they can become familiar and more at ease with the scientific environment and surroundings ahead of time.

5 A period of relaxation and rest was enjoyed by all the participants at the end of the laboratory tests when all the measurements had been finally completed.

6 Some volunteers developed a minor and insignificant localised skin irritation or discomfort to the skin in one place only from wearing the heart monitors, but this went away on its own and without any form of medical treatment.

Activity 9 Phrasal verbs

You saw in Unit 1 that using phrasal verbs can help to increase your general fluency. Complete the following sentences by choosing a phrasal verb from the box. Note that in question 6 the two parts of the phrasal verb are separated by the object of the verb ('the project').

dropped off	took back	measured out	pick up
switched off	carried out	taking part	cut back
worn off	fell through	see through	

1 The hospital sent a taxi to _____ volunteers from their homes.
2 The technician _____ all the equipment before leaving the room.
3 Our plans to continue our studies _____ when the professor would not approve our research proposal.
4 Mrs King _____ her criticisms of my project and said she was happy for me to go ahead after all.
5 The relaxation period after the physical tests was so relaxing that some volunteers _____ to sleep.
6 Professor Sunder said he would postpone his retirement in order to _____ the project _____ to the end.
7 Fifty interviews were _____ in a single day.
8 Davina did not feel any pain after her operation, even when the anaesthetic had _____.
9 Eduardo realised he would have to _____ on time spent at the gym in order to have more time for his coursework.
10 Lucas used to be shy about speaking in a group, but as he became more confident he enjoyed _____ in seminars and discussions.
11 The nurse _____ the medication carefully before administering it to the baby.

Activity 10 University gym survey

Do you ever use a sports or leisure centre? How happy are you with the atmosphere, equipment and facilities? If you could improve the facilities in just one way, what would you do?

A Students' Union conducted research during one day last month to find out what students thought of the university gym. Here are the results of the 110 questionnaires they received.

The staff are pleasant and approachable: Agree 93% Disagree 7%

The staff are knowledgeable and well-trained: Agree 92% Disagree 8%

There is a wide range of fitness classes on offer: Agree 91% Disagree 9%

The fitness classes help me achieve my aims: Agree 97% Disagree 3%

The gym provides a good range of equipment: Agree 88% Disagree 12%

The equipment is modern and well-maintained: Agree 53% Disagree 47%

The standard of cleanliness in the gym is good: Agree 21% Disagree 79%

The showers and changing room facilities at the gym are good: Agree 15% Disagree 85%

Overall, I think the gym provides good value for money: Agree 60% Disagree 40%

1 **Read the results of the survey and decide on the three most important things to improve at the gym.**

2 **Using the information from the survey, write a short report about the gym for the Students' Union. Add any further details required. At the end of the report, make recommendations for ways to improve the gym. Remember to set out the report clearly, under headings, with bullets and/or numbered points. Be concise, use a formal style and summarise some of the statistics using approximations. (Look back over this part of the unit if you want to remind yourself of any of these aspects of writing a report.)**

Activity 11   Spelling

Using the 'look, say, cover, write' spelling method will improve your spelling power.

1   Look carefully at a word and break it into syllables e.g. 'disadvantage' has four syllables – *dis/ad/van/tage*. 'Transmit' has two syllables – *trans/mit* – and 'seminar' has three syllables – *sem/i/nar.*

2   Cover the word with a piece of paper.

3   Move the paper so you see the first syllable only. Study the syllable carefully, photographing it in your mind and saying the syllable to yourself.

4   Move the paper along so you can see the next syllable. Repeat the process until you have mentally 'photographed' the whole word.

5   Cover the word again and write it from memory.

6   Check your spelling with the original. If your spelling was correct, write out the word three times. If you did not get it right, repeat the whole process. Use the word as much as you can to engrave it on your memory.

Activity 12   Adding the suffix *-ity*

The suffix *-ity* is often added to adjectives to make a noun. For example, *major* becomes *majority*. If a noun ends with 'e', the 'e' is dropped when we add *-ity* (e.g. *obese* becomes *obesity*).

1 **All the nouns in the box have been used in this unit. Make sure you understand their meaning and how to pronounce them. Write the adjective each noun comes from. Then use the spelling method explained above to learn to spell them.**

minority	abnormality	publicity	majority
popularity	obesity		

2 **Now choose three of the adjectives you have written and use them in sentences of your own to show their meaning.**

PART 2 WRITING QUESTIONNAIRES

Activity 13   Designing questions for a questionnaire

You are aware that questionnaires are an important part of surveys. Although questionnaires vary a great deal in complexity, all questionnaires need to be worded very carefully to make the results valid.

Hints and tips for writing questionnaires

- Use simple language that everyone can understand.
- Ask clearly targeted questions requiring short answers.
- Do not use open-ended questions which encourage long answers e.g. 'Tell us your thoughts on sport.'
- Do not ask personal questions unless necessary. For example, questions about how much a respondent earns should only be asked if it is essential.
- Do not use 'leading questions' which influence the respondent e.g. 'Do you agree that people are lazier than they used to be?'

1 **Read these extracts from a questionnaire about the use of a university sports centre.**

Sports Centre Customer Satisfaction Survey

1 Which is your age group?

Under 21   ☐

21–45   ☐

46–65   ☐

Over 65   ☐

2 Which facilities do you use? Tick as many as you wish.

Sauna   ☐

Swimming pool   ☐

Gym   ☐

Squash courts   ☐

Basketball courts ☐

Fitness classes   ☐

3 'I would recommend the sports centre to another member of the university.'

Agree   ☐

Disagree   ☐

4 Do you intend to renew your membership at the sports centre next term?

Yes   ☐

No   ☐

5 Please rate your satisfaction with the service at the sports centre on a scale of 1 to 10, with 1 being highly dissatisfied and 10 being highly satisfied. ☐

6 Please add any comments about the sports centre in the box below.

---

2 Use this checklist to evaluate the questionnaire.

a   The language used is simple and straightforward. Yes/No

b   There are personal questions which could cause offence. Yes/No

c   There are leading questions which could influence the respondent. Yes/No

d   There are open-ended questions which might encourage very long responses. Yes/No

e   The questions are specific and show the degree of accuracy required. Yes/No

f   In Question 1 the different age groups are given clearly. Yes/No

g   Question 2 allows multiple responses. Yes/No

h   There is an opportunity to give general views. Yes/No

Activity 14   Asking precise questions

For some surveys it is very important to ask precise questions which will generate answers with specific information.

1   Decide which of the following questions from a survey about tennis would give precise information about the length of time the respondent has been playing tennis.

A When did you start playing tennis?

or

B For how many years/months have you been actively playing tennis?

Years ☐ Months ☐

B is preferable because A could generate too many different answers.

Respondents could answer: … *when I decided to lose weight … a few months ago … recently … when I started secondary school … after my seventeenth birthday … when we could afford the lessons … I started when I was young, but gave up and started again at university … when I decided to get fit … etc.*

2   Choose the more precise question A or B from these pairs.

1A   Why did you take up the sport?

1B   From the list below, please select the top three reasons you took up the sport.

  a) For weight control

  b) For general fitness

  c) To meet new friends

  d) To gain a new sporting skill

  e) Other (please specify)

2A   If a friend or member of your family wanted to take up the sport, how likely would you be to encourage them? Please rate your views on this scale of 1 to 10 where 1 = extremely unlikely and 10 = extremely likely.

  1 2 3 4 5 6 7 8 9 10

2B   On a scale of 1 to 10, would you encourage someone to take an interest in the sport?

Activity 15   Leading questions

1 Decide which of these questions is more likely to influence the respondent.

A Please add any general comments about your experience of tennis in the box below.

B Most people have had some issues with the game. Please add any comments in the box below.

2 **Try to improve these questions.**

1 Don't you agree that people are not as interested in tennis as they used to be?

2 Where do you play tennis?

3 In a typical month, how many times do you play tennis?

Fewer than 3 times	☐
3 to 5 times	☐
5 to 8 times	☐
More than 10	☐

4 How much tennis are you going to play in future?

Activity 16 Designing a questionnaire

1 **Design a short questionnaire to find out what students think of a local sports facility.**

• Think about the sort of things you want to find out e.g. how often they use the facility, whether it is good value for money, whether they would recommend it to a friend.

• Decide how many questions you want to ask.

• Plan the questions carefully and think about their design.

• Remember to avoid leading questions and unnecessary personal questions.

• Look back over this part of the unit for reminders of how to design a good questionnaire.

2 **Write a first draft of your questionnaire. Try the draft on a few friends or family members first. You may then want to modify the questionnaire before using it on a larger sample of people. If you are carrying out a survey with people you don't know, don't do the survey on your own or in a deserted place and don't give any of your own details.**

Now complete your survey.

Activity 17   Writing a report

When you have completed your survey and analysed the data, write a short report recommending ways in which the sports facility could attract more students. Write at least 250 words.

When you write your report, set it out in a clear report format and use a reasonably formal style. Look back at Unit 1 for more information on writing a report.

UNIT 3 Writing a for-and-against essay

In this unit you will practise evaluating the arguments for and against current topics in science and technology. You will also learn how to put forward a logical argument in an essay. Part 1 focuses on organ transplants and animal experiments. Part 2 explores developments in genetic research.

PART 1 WRITING ABOUT ORGAN TRANSPLANTS AND ANIMAL EXPERIMENTS

Activity 1   Brainstorming ideas

1 Read the information about organ transplants.

Make sure you understand:

- what kinds of organs are transplanted
- where the organs come from
- who receives a transplant
- how successful transplant operations are.

Organ transplants

Organ transplants take place when a person (the recipient) is given a new heart, liver, kidney or another major organ because their own organ is failing.

The transplanted organ usually comes from someone who has recently died. This person may be an 'organ donor' – someone who has decided before they died to donate their organs after death to be used for someone else. Sometimes the person was not an organ donor. In that case, permission is given by the person's family.

Alternatively, some organs like kidneys come from a living person. This person is often a close family member who decides to make the sacrifice.

An organ transplant is a serious operation. Sometimes transplant operations are completely successful and sometimes they are unsuccessful. Occasionally a transplant patient dies.

Are organ transplants right or wrong in your view?

To answer a question like this, it is helpful to *brainstorm* – to write down all your ideas uncritically and quickly, even if they seem mad at first.

2 Brainstorm your ideas about organ transplants. You might want to do this by dividing a page into two sections and putting 'pros' (for) on one side and 'cons' (against) on the other side. This will help you organise your ideas later.

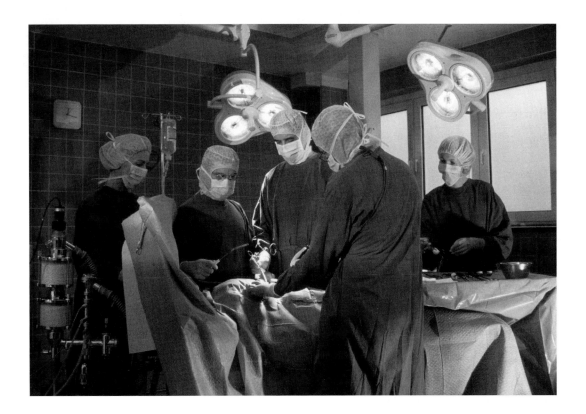

Activity 2 Understanding the question

1 Read this essay question about organ transplants and underline the key words.

Organ transplants are costly and do not always work. However, research into, and operations involving, organ transplants are increasing. This is a waste of time and money.

Write an essay evaluating this opinion.

Evaluating means saying what other people think and giving an answer saying what you think.

2 Now answer these questions.

a   What is the topic of the essay?

b   What do you have to do in the essay? Put this in your own words.

Activity 3 Making a plan

This is a good essay structure for a for-and-against essay where you have to say how far you agree or disagree with an opinion:

- Introduction – say whether you agree or disagree.
- Main part – each paragraph should assess an argument for and against the opinion.
- Conclusion – confirm your views and sum up the arguments.

Pedro has organised ideas for and against organ transplants into the lists below. Were any of his ideas similar to yours? Write 'For' and 'Against' at the top of the correct columns.

Introduction	
• Organ transplants save lives. • Making the parent or child well is good for the whole family. • After the operation people can return to normal lives. • Success rate after operations is fast improving – new techniques/drugs now available. • Organ donation helps a bereaved family to help others. • Research into organ transplants increases all medical knowledge so unrelated areas of health also benefit. • Making use of healthy organs makes sense – they are no use to a person who has died.	• Some patients die soon after a transplant operation. • Some people continue to be very unwell after surgery. • Surgery is stressful – it is better to have a shorter life without this stress. • Medical research into organ transplants is too time-consuming and expensive. • Money spent on organ donation should be spent on researching common illnesses so that the results would benefit more people. • It is wrong to interfere with a dead body or the body's natural process.
Conclusion	

Activity 4 Using linking words

Here are some words and expressions that you can use to introduce and link ideas.

Disagreeing with ideas
It is claimed that ...
It is even/also claimed that ...
People/The opponents of ... say ...
We are told ... but ...

Rejecting ideas
There is a little validity in this argument but ...
This may be true/valid to some extent but ...
Although there is some truth in this, ...
It is true that ... but ...

Contrast expressions
However, ...
Nevertheless, ...
On the other hand, ...
.... but ...
Whereas ...

Opinion
I think/believe/feel that ...
As I see it, ...
In my opinion, ...

Additional points
In addition, ...
Moreover, ...
Furthermore ...
Also/And ...
Another/A further point ...

Sequencing
First, ..., secondly, ...
In the first place, ..., in the second place ...
Finally, ...

Example
For example, ...
For instance, ...
Such as ...

Conclusion
To conclude, ...
To sum up, ...
In conclusion, ...
There are more advantages/benefits than
    disadvantages/drawbacks.
The benefits outweigh the drawbacks.

Activity 5 Evaluating arguments

This is Pedro's essay on organ donation. Read the main part of the essay and notice how the expressions in italics evaluate (give answers to) opinions.

Firstly, *it is often claimed that* organ transplants are not worthwhile because many patients die soon after their operation or survive with a poor quality of life.

There is some validity in this argument but many transplant patients recover well and enjoy a much better quality of life. They are able to take part in family life, return to work or school and do sport or other activities. In addition, when a sick child or parent recovers well, the whole family benefits.

A further point made against transplants is that it would be better for sick people to enjoy the time they have left without the stress of operations. *It is true that* some people would prefer to be left alone to die, *but* many others are prepared to undergo the operation if it gives them a chance of good health. Moreover, new drugs and techniques to help recovery are being developed all the time and the success rate is improving.

1 Complete Pedro's next paragraph choosing the most suitable words in italics.

Thirdly, *people claim/I feel that* that it is wrong to ask families to agree to donate the organs of a loved one who has died *because/but* it increases their grief. *However/Moreover*, families say donating the organs of a loved one is a positive experience *as/although* the organs are not being wasted and are giving the precious gift of life to someone.

2 Complete the paragraph using words from the box. Some words need a capital letter.

the opponents of organ transplants say	while it is true that
they argue that	such as

Finally, _____ that medical research is too expensive and only helps a small number of people. _____ it would be better to direct funding into researching more common illnesses. _____ relatively few people ever need organ transplants, organ transplant research has brought many benefits to unrelated health issues _____ diabetes and cancer.

Activity 6 Writing an introduction

Pedro has written a good introduction. It recycles some of the question in his own words to show he understands what is required.

Underline the expression he uses to explain what he is going to do in the essay.

Organ transplantation is a subject which arouses very strong and emotional views. In this essay, I aim to show why I am in favour of organ transplant operations, even though the procedures are complex and success is not guaranteed.

Activity 7 Writing a conclusion

A conclusion sums up the earlier arguments and says very clearly what you really think.

Choose the best conclusion and say why you think that one is better.

A In conclusion, I have shown that the costs involved in organ transplants are worthwhile because of the ways we can benefit. Moreover, breakthroughs gained from the cutting edge of organ research are of value, not only to those in need of organ donation, but to medicine as a whole.

B To sum up, I have taken this opportunity to discuss the question of organ transplants. There will always be people who agree or disagree with the expense and resources involved in the operations, and it is up to each of us to decide what we think is right.

Activity 8 Medical vocabulary

Match the words in the box with the definitions below.

anaesthetic	anti-rejection drugs	recipient	donor
hormone	arteries and veins	bereaved	plastic surgeon
wound	ethical	graft	disfigured

1 A type of drug given to prevent pain during an operation.
2 These drugs are crucial for the success of organ transplants.
3 Someone who gives an organ.
4 Used to describe a person whose face has been very badly damaged.
5 A chemical substance produced in the body. Two examples are oestrogen and testosterone.
6 Someone who receives an organ.
7 An issue which raises moral arguments. Experimenting on living beings is this kind of issue.
8 Blood flows through these vessels.
9 A doctor who operates on patients to change outward or cosmetic appearance.
10 This needs to heal before the patient is well again.
11 Used to describe someone who is grieving after someone they love has died.
12 The process of surgically joining living tissue from one part of the body to another part.

Activity 9 Capital letters and full stops

A sentence starts with a capital letter and ends with a full stop. Add the capital letters and full stops to the paragraph below.

scientists are now able to experiment on animals using a transgene, which is a gene that has been altered in some way most transgenes are inserted into farm animals to improve their natural traits it is claimed that transgenic techniques mean more precise and cost-effective breeding the opponents of transgenic methods say that the technology is unethical and should not be allowed because of the terrible effects it might have

Activity 10 Commas

Commas are used to separate words in a list, to separate two clauses, and after introductory phrases.

Add the commas in these sentences.

1 People often want plastic surgery for cosmetic not medical reasons.
2 Research involving animals has resulted in successful heart surgery joint replacements organ transplants and drugs for cancer and diabetes.
3 If we are going to find a cure for HIV we need to know what causes the disease.

4   All the clinical studies with the exception of the study on diabetes involved human volunteers.

5   To sum up health education and improved sanitation are the best ways of avoiding disease.

Activity 11   Using an outline – essay on facial transplants

Unfortunately, some people are born with an abnormal appearance or are disfigured through an accident. How do you think this may affect them and their opportunities?

A facial transplant is a type of transplant surgery in which the donor's whole face is grafted on to the recipient's face. Do you think complete transplants are the answer to the problem of facial abnormalities?

1   First read this essay question and underline the key words.

Facial transplants are wrong. The face has too much importance to be suitable for such an extreme form of surgery.

Write an essay evaluating this opinion.

2   Now brainstorm ideas on the pros and cons of facial transplants. Do this before you read the lists below. It is important to work out your own ideas first.

3   Read the lists below. Are any of your ideas here? Tick them off. Add any ideas of your own.

Pros	Cons
People with facial abnormalities can suffer social discrimination.	Upsetting to the bereaved family who know the recipient has the facial characteristics of their loved one.
Facial transplants give the opportunity to live a normal life.	Could be abused by people who want to look more attractive or glamorous.
They help people disfigured in accidents or by illness.	Unknown psychological impact on recipients of no longer having their own face.
The recipient will keep their own bone structure – so will not look exactly like the donor.	Medical ethics – it's wrong – the face is an expression of an individual's personality so should not be transplanted.

4   Choose some of the points from your brainstorm and the list above and develop them into two paragraphs, evaluating the opinion in the essay question. Write between 150 and 200 words.

Activity 12   A for-and-against essay – experiments on animals

1   Read this question. Brainstorm and plan your answer as you did in Activity 11.

Medical experiments on animals are essential if medicine is to progress. The suffering of animals used in experiments is therefore justifiable.

How far do you agree or disagree with this opinion?

2   Add your ideas to this list.

•   Animal experiments have led to many discoveries/increased understanding (e.g. of blood circulation, lung function, role of hormones, etc.).

•   Animals in research are cared for well (anaesthetics, good facilities, etc.).

•   Animals in research have miserable, unnatural lives.

•   Animal research methods are mostly hidden from public knowledge.

3 Develop your argument into two connected paragraphs. Refer to the linking words on page 30.

Activity 13 Proofreading

Brima has written a good answer to the question in Activity 12. There is one mistake in each sentence. Find it and correct it.

Medical experimentation on animal arouses many strong views in this essay, I am going to show that, although animal research has led to medical advances such as the polio vaccine and heart transplants, overall it is cruel and unnecessary.

In the first one, it is argued that animal research has led to important advances in medical understanding such as blood circulation and the role of hormones. While there may be some truth in this, we do not need using animals in experiments these days, as we have alternative research methods, including computer modelling and robotics.

Secondly, scientists say animals in research are cared for well and that they are gave anaesthetics and good food. However, ordinary citizens they do not know for sure what goes on in laboratories. It could be that animals suffer immensely and dying in great pain.

Furthermore, although we are told us that animal experiments are being improved, new developments in transgenic methods have increased the suffering of animals. A dog, for example, may be given jeans from a cow, which can lead to terrible effects on the dog.

To sum up, although it is true that medical experiments on animals have led to treatments and cures for some illnesses, modern developments mean their are better alternative methods available. In my view, animal experiments should be reduce and eventually stopped completely.

You already know that an essay needs a clear structure. Remember Pedro used the structure:

- Introduction – say whether you agree or disagree.
- Main part – each paragraph should assess an argument for and against the opinion.
- Conclusion – confirm your views and sum up the arguments.

Did Brima use this structure?

Activity 14 Relative pronouns

The relative pronoun *who* refers to a person or people, whereas *which* refers to a thing or things. For example:

*The doctor operated on a patient **who** was very ill.*

*This is a new machine **which** patients can use at home to check their blood pressure.*

Whose is used instead of *his/her/their*.

Other relative pronouns are:

- *where* – to refer to a place
- *when* – to refer to a time
- *why* – to refer to a reason
- *what* – meaning 'the thing which'.

1 Join the following pairs of sentences into one sentence using a relative pronoun.

a There is the chest clinic. Heart transplants are carried out there.

b Marisa works in a clinic. It does not charge patients who cannot afford to pay.

c   I work with a woman. Her daughter is training to be a brain surgeon in Milan.

d   October 1st is an important anniversary. We celebrate my father's recovery from surgery on that day.

e   Every day, I drive past the hospital. All my children were born there.

f   We never found out the name of the person. He saved my brother from drowning.

g   The nurse examined the wound. It was about 10 centimetres long but not very deep.

h   A general anaesthetic is not used on patients. Their medical history makes it inappropriate.

i   Skin grafting is a specialised technique. It works particularly well in the case of burns victims.

2   Use *who*, *why*, *when*, *which*, *what* and *whose* in these sentences.

a   Nurses/give/pain-relieving drugs/any patients/appear to be/pain.

b   Are/you/go/destroy/medicines/out of date?

c   I want/help/mother/child/needed a bone marrow transplant.

d   We carry out research/find out/people develop the disease.

e   Is that/room/all the equipment/sterilised?

f   Good patients do/the doctor tells them.

g   Can you understand/those people are saying?

Activity 15   Academic style – tone and register

Read the expressions in the box and delete any which would not sound right in an academic essay.

My granddad believes …	Studies carried out by the United Nations show …
According to the biotechnology associations …	That problem has never bothered me …
I was watching something on TV which said …	Recent medical statistics indicate …
Loads of my friends think …	It's going to be ages before …
Experts agree …	It's a bit scary …
You shouldn't always believe what you read in the papers …	

PART 2 WRITING ABOUT GENETIC RESEARCH

Activity 16   Specialised vocabulary

Match the specialised terms in the box to the definitions.

gene	genetic diagnosis	gene therapy	hereditary disease

1   The unit of DNA containing the hereditary material in a cell.

2   This technique involves treating genetic disease by replacing faulty genes with functioning genes so the body can repair itself.

3   Parents who worry they may pass on a disease to their unborn children may ask for this.

4   An illness or condition you are born with.

Activity 17   Discussing genetic techniques

In pairs or small groups, explore your views on the following issues. (Look at the correct answers to Activity 16 for help with the specialist vocabulary.)

1   Some people who know they might pass on an inherited health condition to their unborn child may decide to have a genetic diagnosis to assess the level of risk. Other people in the same position may decide against this. Why do you think some potential parents might refuse a genetic diagnosis?

2   Having repeated gene therapy treatments has cured some patients suffering from genetic diseases. However, in other cases, gene therapy has failed. Discuss some possible reasons why gene therapy might not be successful.

3   In the future, employers might ask job applicants for a genetic diagnosis before giving them a job. Do you think this is reasonable? What are your views?

Activity 18   Analysing a model essay

1 Look at this essay question about genetic research. Read it and underline what the question is asking you to do.

It is often said that genetic research in medicine will find cures for many illnesses, but the truth is, overall, the research is likely to do more harm than good.

How far do you agree or disagree with this opinion?

2 Write an answer of at least 250 words.

3 Read the way Maryam has approached this essay question below and then answer these questions.

- Is the argument in favour of genetic research in medicine? Yes/No
- Is the argument easy to follow with some clear reasons and examples? Yes/No
- Is the essay divided into paragraphs? Yes/No
- Is there a different topic in each paragraph? Yes/No
- Is there a clear introduction which says how the question will be answered? Yes/No
- Does the conclusion follow logically from the argument? Yes/No
- Is the conclusion realistic? Yes/No
- Are the grammar, spelling and punctuation good? Yes/No
- Is the tone of the essay reasonably formal? Yes/No
- Is the structure the same one used by Pedro and Brima? Yes/No

It is often argued that genetic research in medicine is not valid because the consequences are unknown. In this essay, I am going to show that there are many advantages to genetic research and that, overall, the benefits to people outweigh the drawbacks.

Firstly, people say that gene therapy should not be used because it is at an experimental stage and the consequences for patients are uncertain. While it is true that the research is still in relatively early stages, gene therapy patients are always informed of the risks. They undergo the procedures of their own free will.

In second place, it is argued that gene therapy is very unpleasant and stressful for patients. This may be true, but once the treatment has finished, patients may have a complete cure with no ill-effects at all. In addition, gene therapy might avoid the need for dangerous operations because diseased organs may be able to repair themselves.

An argument used against genetic diagnosis is that it could put parents in an impossible dilemma. Parents who might pass on disabling conditions will have to choose whether to have children or not. However, surely most of us would prefer to be informed about the consequences of our actions? A genetic diagnosis means that parents who decide to have children are better prepared for the future.

Finally, it is claimed that genetic research will lead to discrimination against individuals. For example, it is said that if employers find out from an applicant's gene profile that he has a possibility of developing cancer, he will not be offered the job. My view is that new laws to protect the genetic privacy of the individual would resolve these problems.

To sum up, I think the potential benefits of genetic research make the risks and expense justifiable, so I strongly disagree with the opinion in the question. Science is on the threshold of significant discoveries about how our genes work which might bring an end to many disabling conditions. As long as we have legal safeguards to protect the privacy of the individual, I feel optimistic about the future.

4 **This sentence is missing from Maryam's essay. Draw a line on the essay to show where it should go.**

Moreover, it is thought insurance companies will refuse to insure those who have been told they are going to develop a hereditary disease.

Activity 19   Confusing words

Choose the correct word from each pair.

1 Poverty is the *route/root* cause of many problems.

2 The psychological *effects/affects* of the operation were far-reaching.

3 The genome contains all the hereditary material in the *sell/cell*.

4 Good health is said by most people to be *priceless/worthless*.

5 Even if the treatment does him not cure him, it cannot do him any *harm/injury*.

6 Undergoing a dangerous operation was preferable to suffering *intolerable/intolerant* pain.

7 In 30 years of improved life expectancy only 10% is due to medical advances.
   Nevertheless/Furthermore, funding for medical research continues to grow rapidly.

8 The nurse will *assess/access* patients before the doctor sees them.

9 The committee provides *advice/advise* on medical ethics.

10 At the moment the treatment is in the early stages. *However/Moreover,* by the end of the next decade it will have become routine.

Activity 20   Capital letters

Capital letters are used for proper nouns.

Mark the words in the box which should have capital letters.

genetic engineering	bacteria
organ transplants	carbon dioxide
selective breeding	tb
agriculture	australian foundation for birth defects
easter	november
cystic fibrosis	antibiotics
new york college of science and engineering	united nations
tallinn	autumn
professor garcia	chinese centre for technology strategy
plastic surgeon	alzheimer's disease
tuesday	ramadan
atlantic ocean	marie curie

Activity 21   Genetically modified (GM) food

1 **Read this essay question about genetically modified (GM) food. Make sure you understand what you are being asked to write about. Write a minimum of 250 words.**

Genetically modified (GM) food will improve food and consumer choice. There is no valid reason why anyone should object to these exciting developments in the food industry. How far do you agree or disagree with this opinion?

2 **You will need to brainstorm your ideas. You can use the list of points below to add to your brainstorm. Make sure you put them under the correct headings – 'For' or 'Against'.**

- GM food unnatural/might be unhealthy/lead to illness in future.

- GM food tasty/more food products/more consumer choice.

- New development – no long-term studies on effects on people/farmland/growers.

- Food not 'natural' nowadays anyway. GM techniques no worse than other technological/ scientific methods to grow and preserve food.

- Supermarkets label GM food – consumers aware/make up own minds.

Here is a summary of the steps you should go through when writing your essay.

- Brainstorm ideas – decide whether you are for or against GM food.
- Select best ideas.
- Write paragraphs assessing pros and cons of issues.
- Write a suitable introduction and conclusion.
- Check:
  - the content – is the information sensible?
  - the structure – is it well-organised with an effective introduction and conclusion?
  - are the ideas linked clearly with suitable linking expressions?
  - language – are the spelling, punctuation and grammar correct?
  - register – is it formal?
- Write a second draft, incorporating your corrections.

3 Read these essay questions. Make sure you understand what you are being asked to write about and then write a minimum of 250 words on each one. (Look back at Activities 9, 16 and 18 for vocabulary on genetic research methods.)

1 *Life would be better without mobile phones. What is your view?*

2 *Transgenic methods result in superior farm animals who are more productive. There is no reason why anyone should object to the obvious benefits this has for both the farmer and the consumer. Discuss.*

3 *Genetic research holds the best hope for the future of human medicine. It is only right that funding for genetic research should dramatically increase. How far do you agree or disagree with this statement?*

4 *GM techniques are our main hope for the end of world hunger. How far do you support this view?*

5 *There is nothing wrong with having cosmetic surgery to look good. Discuss.*

UNIT 4   Writing problem-solving essays

In this unit you will learn to write well-organised essays suggesting solutions to problems. The unit is divided into two parts:

- Part 1 focuses on writing essays about environmental issues.
- Part 2 focuses on writing essays about social problems.

PART 1 WRITING ABOUT ENVIRONMENTAL ISSUES

Activity 1   Environmental issues

 What do you think are the most important environmental issues today? What do you think can be done about these issues?

1 Read this short report about global warming and then answer these questions.

a   What is global warming?

b   What causes it?

c   What are the possible effects?

d   What can be done to stop global warming?

Global warming

Scientific research suggests that global warming, defined as the increase in the average world temperature, is a reality.

Many scientists now believe that *pollution* by certain gases, especially carbon dioxide *emissions*, is one of the main causes of global warming. Industrialised countries produce more carbon emissions per person than less developed countries.

Although global warming may have some possible benefits, such as milder winters in some countries, on the whole global warming is considered to be a *threat* to the environment.

The negative consequences of global warming include unpredictable weather patterns, *drought*, increased rainfall, and flooding. Moreover, the *polar ice caps* have shown signs of *melting* and are causing rising sea levels. A large rise in the number of mosquitoes is also expected, increasing the problem of malaria.

To control global warming, there is a need to reduce pollution from *fossil fuels*. Rising demand for energy can be met by exploring *renewable sources of energy*. More efficient *recycling* will also help reduce global warming.

2 Match the definitions to the words in italics in the report.

a   Energy that comes from the wind, sun, tides or waves.

b   Areas around the North or South Poles.

c   Turning from a solid to a liquid due to heat.

d   Gases sent into the air.

e   A long period without rain.

f   Processing materials like glass, paper, wood or plastic to use again.

g   Coal, gas or oil burned for energy.

h   Something that could do harm.

i   Damage to the environment from harmful substances.

Activity 2   Brainstorming ideas

1 Study this essay question and underline the key words. Make sure you understand the question and what you have to do.

Global warming is a serious problem. What measures could be taken by governments and individuals to help control global warming and reduce its harmful effects?

The question requires you to think of solutions that could be taken by governments and individuals to control global warming.

2 Brainstorm solutions on the topic. The question has two parts so divide your paper into two sections.

* Personal solutions to global warming e.g. choose a fuel-efficient car, walk or cycle instead of driving.

* Government solutions to global warming e.g. develop solar, wind, wave and tidal sources of energy.

3 Marcus has brainstormed the points below to answer the essay question. Read his list of points. Are they the same as yours?

Personal solutions
- Cut waste and recycle.
- Cut energy consumption – choose small, fuel-efficient cars.
- Make home more energy-efficient – reduce heat loss through roof insulation, etc.
- Encourage friends and family to take similar action.

Government solutions
- Develop solar, wind, wave and tidal sources of energy.
- Provide recycling facilities.
- Monitor output from power stations.
- Fund research into climate change.
- Sign international agreements to reduce emissions.

4 Here are some more solutions to the problem of global warming. Decide whether they are personal solutions or government solutions. One point is not relevant to the topic and you should ignore that point.
- Reduce use of air conditioner/adjust thermostat by a few degrees.
- Improve public awareness through educational campaigning.
- Increase budget allocated for research into space exploration.

Activity 3 Reading and understanding an essay

1 Here is a paragraph from the main part of Marcus's essay. Underline the words he uses to make suggestions.

At a personal level, individuals, in my view, should take action to solve the problems of climate change. One solution is to make homes more energy-efficient. For example, heat loss could be reduced by roof insulation. In hot weather, people could adjust the thermostat of the air conditioner by a few degrees. Another solution is to use 'greener' transport, people could buy small, fuel-efficient cars. In addition, people can cut down on waste. Reducing the amount we buy, for instance, or recycling items would all help save energy.

2 Read the next paragraph from Marcus's essay and fill in the gaps using the words in the box. Some words need a capital letter.

| one solution | an additional solution | moreover, |
| finally | can | could |

Secondly, at a national and international level, governments should implement ways to reduce pollution. _____ is to set targets for the reduction of carbon dioxide emissions. Governments _____ monitor the output from power stations, for example, to ensure pollution levels are as low as possible. _____ is to develop alternative sources of energy such as wind power. _____ governments _____ support local people by improving public transport and recycling facilities. _____ I believe governments should sign international agreements promising to cut carbon emissions.

Activity 4   Essay structure

An essential structure for a problem-solving essay is:

- Introduction – refer to the question and say how you will approach solving the problem given in the question.
- Main text – suggest solutions to the problem with reasons and examples. If the question has two elements e.g. individual/government solutions, cover each element in separate paragraphs. The number of main paragraphs depends on the length of the essay. Two main paragraphs are usually needed for an essay of about 250 words.
- Conclusion – sum up the solutions outlined in the main text and point to the future in a positive and realistic way.

1   Here is Marcus's introduction. It is good because he refers to the question and says how he is going to answer it. Add the punctuation and capital letters to the introduction.

finding solutions to global warming is essential if we are to protect the environment in my view the most effective approach is for governments and individuals to work together to find solutions in this essay i am going to show how we can all take responsibility to protect the earth for ourselves and future generations

2   Good conclusions for problem-solving essays sum up solutions, sound positive, and may point to the future in a realistic way. Choose the best conclusion from the two conclusions below and say why you chose that one.

A In conclusion, global warming is a serious problem that we cannot afford to ignore. Individuals can make a difference by the lifestyle they choose, and they can also spread the message to friends and family. As I outlined earlier, I also believe governments should cooperate to research the problem, nationally and internationally, and continue to look for the most effective solutions.

B To conclude, global warming has been going on for a long time and may have caused disasters such as hurricanes and flooding. In future, we may see worldwide starvation if crops fail due to drought. It is probably too late now to do anything much about climate change. However, if governments introduced a 'green tax' on everyone immediately, there might be some hope.

Activity 5   Word combinations

Two or more words can be combined to make new expressions. For example, *global* + *warming* gives us *global warming* and *global* + *village* gives us *global village* (the idea that global communication is now as easy as communication in a village due to advances in telecommunications).

Here are some more word combinations, some of which are used in Marcus's essay.

green tax	tidal power	nuclear energy	ozone layer
fossil fuels	carbon sinks	wind farm	acid rain
carbon footprint	greenhouse effect		

Word combinations may be separate words, joined up or joined by a hyphen e.g. life jacket, lifeboat, life-threatening.

Match each of the sentences below with a word combination from the box.

1   This causes damage wherever it falls into forests, lakes and the soil.

2   This prevents dangerous radiation from the sun reaching us.

3   This is a renewable form of energy from the oceans.

4   This is a way of measuring the individual's impact on the environment.

5   This is what we call the build-up of gases which cannot escape from the earth.

6   These giant turbines can generate electricity from wind power.

7   This is a charge imposed by governments to protect the environment.

8   The waste from this form of power is very dangerous.

9   These things absorb carbon in a harmless way.

10 Oil, coal and gas are examples of these.

Activity 6   Linking ideas

These sentence halves have been jumbled. Match the separate halves of each sentence so the full sentences make sense.

1   Although wind farms have become a popular source of renewable energy, in some areas

by building storm shelters, storing food and water supplies and increasing their insurance cover.

2   As a way of reducing their carbon footprint, businesses are encouraging staff to use company buses rather than drive to work,

will now have to pay a green tax on any profits made from business activities.

3   As well as being important carbon sinks, the rainforests

had destroyed all the plants and insects that once lived there.

4   Local people have prepared for climate change

but many employees are still reluctant to give up their own transport.

5   Even though the lake still looked pure and beautiful, acid rain

are a rich source of medicinal flowers and plants.

6   Companies who want to develop forest areas for business purposes

residents complain of noise vibration and disfigured landscapes.

Activity 7   Suggesting solutions

You have already noticed some phrases to suggest solutions to a problem

e.g. *One solution is **to make homes more energy efficient**.*

You can build up solutions by saying *A further/another/an additional solution is …'*

e.g. *Another solution is **to use 'greener' transport**.*

1   Write further solutions to the situations described below. Use a phrase from the box. The first one has been done for you.

A further solution is	Another solution is	An additional solution is

a   One solution to the problem of deforestation is to plant more trees than are cut down. (control farming/industrial activity/threatened forest areas.)

   One solution to the problem of deforestation is to plant more trees than are cut down. A further solution is to control farming and ban industrial activity in threatened forest areas.

b   One solution to the problem of rising sea levels is to build high sea walls. (move people/ living/coast/homes/further inland.)

c   One solution to prevent more damage from acid rain is to monitor pollution levels in the atmosphere. (impose penalties/emissions/power stations/above acceptable level.)

d   One solution to the problem of drought is to save water in reservoirs. (grow crops/require little water.)

e One solution to limit the depletion of the ozone layer is to have a global agreement banning the use of CFCs in aerosols and refrigerators. (control emissions/nitrous oxide/planes/cars.)

2 Add further solutions to these sentences.

One solution to the issue of waste disposal in cities is to provide regular rubbish collections. A further solution is to _____ .

One solution to the rising demand for food is to develop better varieties of seed. A further solution is to _____ .

Activity 8 Using modal verbs to suggest solutions

Can and *could* are useful words in problem-solving essays. They can be used to make suggestions and recommendations for future action. *Could* is less definite than *can*:

*People **can** cut down on waste.*
*Governments **could** support local people by improving public transport.*

We also use *should* and *ought to* in problem-solving essays to express strong advice:

*Governments **should** implement ways to reduce pollution.*
*Everyone **ought to** take responsibility for the amount of waste they produce.*

Must is even stronger than *should* or *ought to*. It is used when the speaker thinks something is not just advisable but necessary:

*We **must** take action to reverse climate change before it is too late.*

All these verbs are modal verbs. They are used before the infinitive without 'to', except for 'ought to'. *Should, must* and *ought to* are often followed with a practical example to develop the idea. *Can* or *could* are often used in the examples:

*Governments **should** sign international agreements to cut carbon emissions. For example, they **could** agree to impose a green tax on planes using international airspace.*

*Everyone **ought to** take responsibility for the amount of waste they produce. For example, we **can** all try to use fewer plastic carrier bags when we go shopping.*

1 Complete the first sentence in each statement below using *should*, *ought to* or *must*. Then complete the second sentence using *could* or *can*. The first one has been done for you.

a Governments _____ take precautions to prevent radiation poisoning from nuclear waste. For example, it _____ be transported in special containers and disposed of under safe conditions.

  Governments *must* take precautions to prevent radiation poisoning from nuclear waste. For example, it *could* be transported in special containers and disposed of under safe conditions.

b Governments _____ encourage people to protect themselves from the effects of ozone layer depletion. For example, media campaigns _____ emphasise the importance of wearing a sun hat and long sleeves.

c Tourist agencies _____ ensure heritage sites and traditional cultures are not damaged by visitors. For instance, numbers visiting a particular place _____ be limited, and funds raised _____ be used to improve local people's way of life.

d Environmental agencies _____ control coastal erosion. For example, they _____ ban excavation or building developments in sensitive areas.

2 Add your own examples to develop these ideas.

a We should make tourists aware of how they can behave responsibly when they are on holiday. For example, _____ .

b TV advertisements could help make people more aware of ways to conserve water. For instance, _____.

c International agencies should help people affected by earthquakes. For example, _____.

Activity 9 Linking ideas to examples

Use the words in the box to complete the gaps in this paragraph about fishing.

Finally,	Moreover,	However,	also	For example,

Overfishing is seriously depleting the world's stock of fish. _____ there are ways we can protect our fish stocks and ensure a good supply of fish for future generations. _____ governments can set quotas to limit the amount of fish that can be taken out of the oceans. _____ fishing for certain kinds of fish which are in danger of extinction could be stopped completely. To avoid unintentional damage to fish, methods of fishing could _____ be more humane. _____ governments should monitor fishing activity and penalise companies which break the rules.

Activity 10 Writing paragraphs – rural migration

It is important for the structure of an essay to have paragraphs. Each paragraph should introduce a new idea or fact and consist of at least two sentences.

For example, if you were writing an essay on rural migration you would want to have several paragraphs about why rural migration is happening, what the effects of rural migration are, and what can be done about it.

1 Brainstorm your ideas on rural migration. These questions might help you.

- Why has rural migration happened? (For example, the population may have moved from the countryside to the towns in search of work.)

- What are the effects of rural migration on the countryside? (For example, village schools may close and the people left behind may all be elderly.)

- What can be done about rural migration? (One solution is to improve conditions for people in the countryside so they are less likely to want to leave.)

2 Now select ideas from your brainstorm and develop them into at least two paragraphs. You can also choose any points from the box below to use in your paragraphs. Remember to link your paragraphs clearly.

media campaign to improve image of rural life	attract more teachers
encourage businesses into the rural areas	develop rural healthcare
agricultural subsidies for farmers	standard of living
employment schemes	appreciate opportunities
better transport networks	see a positive future
better funding of schools	money to pay for goods and services

Activity 11 Spelling and vocabulary

Changing verbs to nouns

Many verbs can be turned into nouns by adding *-ion* e.g. *solve–solution, pollute–pollution, insulate–insulation*. Note that if the verb ends in *-e*, the final 'e' is dropped before adding *-ion*.

1 Learn to spell these words correctly through the 'look, say, cover, write' spelling method (see Unit 2).

solution	radiation	pollution	emissions
determination	vaccination		

Changing nouns to adjectives

The ending *-al* can be added to nouns to make an adjective e.g. *nation–national, globe–global, tide–tidal*. Note that if the noun ends in *-e*, the final 'e' is dropped before adding *–al*.

2 Learn to spell these adjectives correctly through the 'look, say, cover, write' spelling method.

national	global	tidal	additional	environmental

Activity 12 Academic style – expressing caution

1 Compare these pairs of sentences.

   A Doubling the price of petrol will stop people using their cars.

   B An increase in the price of petrol may reduce car use.

   A Rents should be cut by 75 per cent to help poor people.

   B Reducing rents may be a way of helping low-income families.

The second sentence of each pair (B) is more suitable for academic writing. It sounds more cautious because of the word 'may'. It is also more realistic to suggest modest changes rather than huge changes.

2 Change the style of these sentences in a similar way to the model sentences (B) above.

   a   Cutting the price of food by 80 per cent would prevent poverty.

   b   Increasing the price of tobacco by 90 per cent will make people stop smoking.

   c   Doubling the length of prison sentences would stop crime.

Activity 13 Steps to solving problems

There are several general phrases you can use in an essay to describe steps that can be taken to solve problems.

1 Here is a list of general steps that governments and ordinary citizens can take. Read the phrases carefully, ticking any that you have already used in an essay.

Governments can:

   a   Research and monitor developments and keep relevant statistics.

   b   Cooperate with other countries to find solutions.

   c   Set targets and sign international agreements.

   d   Educate people through the media or schools.

   e   Follow guidelines from respected authorities.

f   Prepare for expected changes by developing the infrastructure.

   g   Impose penalties on organisations that break rules.

   h   Develop strategies in case there is an unexpected crisis.

Ordinary citizens can:

   i   Share ideas for solutions with others.

   j   Volunteer to work on projects organised by local residents.

   k   Follow official advice and change behaviour if necessary.

   l   Stay informed of any developments.

   m   Support or join agencies which work to find solutions.

   n   Set up a campaign for action.

   o   Publicise the problem.

2 Here is a list of examples showing the practical steps that can be taken to solve problems. Each practical step illustrates a general step from the lists above (a to o). Match each practical step to a general step. The first three have been done for you.

   a   People listened to the local radio to get the latest news on the progress of the hurricane.
       General step l: Stay informed of any developments.

   b   Jihad worked with others in his village to build and strengthen the banks of the local river.
       General step j: Volunteer to work on projects organised by local residents.

   c   When a tourist complex was built on farmland without permission, the tourist company had to pay large amounts of money to farmers.
       General step g: Impose penalties on organisations that break rules.

   d   Local officials are asked to count all births and deaths in the area and record the changes in population growth.

   e   People have become more careful about personal hygiene since reading the leaflets about how to stop infectious diseases spreading.

   f   The emergency services followed a well-coordinated plan to evacuate people in the flooded areas safely.

   g   When many people began to migrate to cities, the government built more roads, housing and schools.

   h   Ministers attended an international conference to discuss ways to prevent the spread of malaria.

3 Write an example of a practical step of your own and match it to one of the general steps above.

Activity 14   Writing a problem-solving essay

Choose one of the following essay questions. Remember to read the question carefully first and underline the key words. Use the essay structure in Activity 4. Write a first draft and then proofread it for errors. Then write a second draft. Write at least 250 words.

   1   *Despite warnings from experts, industrial pollution in many places is still increasing. Outline some strategies to limit industrial pollution.*

   2   *Trees are essential to life. However, in many areas deforestation is a serious problem. What can be done to control deforestation?*

   3   *In many countries, the number of cars on the roads continues to increase. How can the impact of car use on the environment be reduced?*

   4   *Earthquakes, famines, hurricanes and other natural disasters cause terrible destruction. Discuss one natural disaster and explore ways to reduce its effects.*

   5   *Choose **one** major health issue such as malaria, TB, HIV or pandemic flu. Consider strategies to address the issue that could be taken nationally, internationally and at an individual level.*

   6   *Although global tourism brings benefits, it has also had some adverse effects. Discuss strategies to limit the negative effects of tourism.*

PART 2 WRITING ABOUT SOCIAL PROBLEMS

Activity 15   Solving the problems of old age

In this activity you will answer an essay question on solving the problems of old age.

1 Before you answer the question, think about older people you know.

- How do they enjoy themselves?
- What, if anything, is difficult for them?
- What have you noticed about the needs of older people?
- What do the Government or official agencies do to meet their needs?

2 Read the essay question and highlight the key words. Make sure you understand the problem and know what the question requires you to do.

Most of us agree that it is important to take account of the needs of older people. What do you think can be done by official agencies to support older people? What could older people do to help themselves?

3 Brainstorm some ways to reduce the problems faced by elderly people. As you have done before, divide the page into two sections and list your ideas.

Remember, the question has two aspects:

- help from official agencies
- actions older people can take to help themselves.

This is Rachel's brainstorm. Are any of your ideas here?

Official agencies solutions:
- develop health services to support age-related conditions e.g. arthritis
- provide goods and services designed for the social and leisure interests of older people
- promote a positive image of older people in the media – useful, wise, serene
- fund research into the needs of older people.

Individual solutions:
- develop new interests
- socialise with others
- learn new skills
- broaden horizons e.g. travel
- take part in family and community life e.g. help with grandchildren or do voluntary work.

4 Rachel also thought of these ideas but only two are relevant to the question. Add the two relevant ideas to your brainstorm.

- Allow older people to stay in their jobs if they want to.
- Avoid contact with chemicals which could be dangerous for health.
- Save for old age/use pension schemes.

Activity 16 Proofreading and correcting an essay

1 Rachel has written a good answer to the question about older people. Proofread her essay carefully and correct the mistakes. There are eight errors to find.

Life expectancy in many countries has been increasing steadily and my friends look forward to their grandparents attending their graduation ceremonies. An increased life expectancy raises there many issues. In this essay, I will outline what elderly people can do to ensure them a good future and also discuss ways official agencies can give support.

In the first place, I believe older people should to expect a tranquil and creative future. One solution to the lack of interest in life suffered by some elderly people is to have new challenges. Positive experiences such as travel will renew their energy. Older people also want to do things for others, so encouraging their to help in charity projects it is very rewarding.

The government can playing a role too, in supporting older people by providing appropriate goods and services. For example, health care and public transport could they be tailored to the needs of the elderly. Furthermore, official bodies can arranging financial help or provide worthwhile pension schemes.

2 Now add the punctuation to Rachel's conclusion.

in conclusion i think that a combination of government planning social support and personal determination will allow older people to live peacefully they should be able to remain deeply interested in life and be free from unnecessary worries

3 How far does Rachel's view of old age reflect your own view? What problems did she not mention and how might they be resolved?

Activity 17 Vocabulary check

Choose the correct word from the pairs of words in italics.

1 Places where crowds *gather/group* may be closed during a pandemic.

2 In the past, people often did not *expect/accept* to be alive to see their first grandchild.

3 *Waist/waste* measurement is now thought to be a better indicator of health than *wait/weight* in kilos.

4 She was warned by her doctor that smoking *depleted/depicted* the body's ability to use Vitamin B.

5 A *balanced/regular* diet includes food from all the major food groups.

Activity 18 The problem of obesity

1 Read this essay question. Highlight the key words. Make sure you understand the issue and what you have to do and then brainstorm some ideas as you did in Activity 15.

In many parts of the world obesity is becoming a health issue. Children in particular are at risk of developing serious obesity-related illnesses later in life.

What can be done by governments and families to limit the increased incidence of obesity in children?

2 One paragraph for the main part of the essay has been partly completed. Complete it and write one or two further main paragraphs (we have given you the start of the second paragraph as well). Then add the introduction and conclusion to complete the essay.

> One solution to the problem of obesity is for the government to make the population aware of the need for a healthy diet. This can be carried out through _____.
> _____. Children could also be taught about nutrition at _____ so that they understand what the body requires in terms of fats, vitamins and proteins. Furthermore, the amount of sport offered at school can be increased. It has been shown, for example, that if children enjoy sport _____ .
> Steps families can take themselves include ...

Activity 19 Vocabulary check – mental health

Read this report about mental health and choose the correct word from each pair of words in italics.

> The World Health Organisation *has/was* predicted that in developed countries depression will become the world's second major illness. Depression is characterised *in/by* loss of interest in life and lack *in/of* motivation.
>
> It is not known exactly what causes depression. Childhood environmental *factors/elements* are thought to influence the *onset/progress* of the illness.
>
> Recent psychological research also suggests that features *of/to* modern life may be to blame for the increasing *incidence/accidents* of depression. There is a lot of rapid change and a faster *pace/state* of life. Families are often less close. In addition, experts say people are less sure of their *role/roll* in life.

(continued)

However, scientists agree that people are designed to find ways to look *for/to* happiness. This basic evolutionary *mechanism/mechanic* protects the human race and *insures/ensures* its survival. In fact, people *who/which* adapt well to change will not only survive but also have a good chance of increasing their capacity *for/of* happiness.

Activity 20   Model essay

1 This essay question is about motivation and personal success. Read the essay question and underline the key words. Make sure you understand the problem and know what the essay requires, then brainstorm some ideas.

An international survey suggested that young people lacked a sense of purpose. The report claimed that young people were less happy today than their grandparents were.

What do you think could help young people improve their motivation?

2 Read Ritesh's essay and then answer the questions.

A sense of purpose is essential to feeling motivated and in control of life. In this essay, I will show what can be done to develop motivation and personal determination.

One solution to lack of motivation is for young people to identify their *unique* qualities and talents. Identifying what we are excellent at doing would provide direction and motivation. When we know our strengths, we can focus on making these skills *marketable* in our future careers.

In addition, parents can play an important role when their children are still young by helping them decide what they want. If children are helped to set goals, and are given praise and some constructive criticism, then children grow up trying harder and will overcome *setbacks*. Working for success becomes a habit.

Furthermore, I believe all goals should be planned and achieved in small stages. For example, my lifelong ambition is to have a career in health care. I *sought* every opportunity I could that would help me reach this goal. Finally, I got a part-time job in a children's hospital helping to feed and wash sick patients. It was a *humble* start, but it helped me win a university place to study medicine.

To conclude, lack of motivation can be overcome when people set goals that are believable and achievable. Family support also helps a great deal. Never give up, as there is always a way forward. I strongly believe in the saying, 'The lift may be out of order, but the stairs are always working.'

a   Is the essay set out clearly with an introduction, main part and conclusion?

b   Does each paragraph deal with separate aspects of the topic?

c   Are the ideas suggested applicable to everyone?

d   Does Ritesh give clear explanations?

e   Are there suitable linking words?

f   Is the style suitable for an academic audience?

g   Are the punctuation, spelling and vocabulary good?

h   Does the essay answer the question?

i   Does the introduction say how the question will be answered?

j   Does the conclusion sum up the arguments and sound realistic?

3 Find words in Ritesh's essay which mean the same as the words or phrases in this list.

- different from everyone and everything else
- looked for
- simple, basic
- problems causing delay
- have commercial value/something people will pay for

4 Make a note of the main topic of each paragraph in Ritesh's essay.

5 Ritesh has personalised the topic of motivation, using pronouns such as *we* and *us*. This is acceptable because he writes about principles which are applicable to all young people. Find two examples of general principles in his essay.

6 What does the quotation in his final sentence mean? How far do you agree with it?

Activity 21   Word building

Complete the sentences with words or parts of words from the box.

back	able	model	market	goal	down	over

1   Anya chose as her role _____ an Olympic gold medallist whose determination was very inspiring.

2   The living conditions in the run _____ apartment block were poor and received an unfavour _____ report by the inspector.

3   He did not succeed at his first job interview, but he did not let this set _____ stop him applying for other opportunities.

4   Alex was unaware that her ability to create delicious dinners for her friends was a highly _____ able skill.

5   Walt Disney _____ came repeated failure to become the most successful film-maker of his generation.

6   Graduates who took part in a detailed _____ setting exercise were found to be earning ten times more in later years than graduates who did not attend the seminar.

Activity 22   Writing a problem-solving essay

1 This essay is about how poverty prevents people from participating in society. Read this essay question and highlight the key words. Make sure you understand the problem and know what the essay requires you to do.

Many people are still too poor to participate fully in society. What can be done to reduce poverty and increase social opportunities?

2 Brainstorm the topic as usual. The words in the box below may trigger some ideas.

training courses	goalsetting	self-discipline	determination
award	role model	self-confidence	study
employer awareness	improve schools	public libraries	
controlled rents/loans	develop poor neighbourhoods	high expectations	

3 Think about and plan your paragraphs, using the essay structure in Activity 4. Start your essay like this.

Many people are affected by social and economic disadvantages which prevent them from being able to develop their lives or benefit from the opportunities others enjoy. However, there are a number of ways these problems can be overcome. In this essay I will show that …

4 Proofread your first draft for mistakes then produce a second draft.

5 Write at least 250 words on one or more of these essay titles.

1 *Research indicates that people over 45 often find it more difficult than young people to get jobs or promotion. How can we address the issue of age discrimination in the workplace?*

2 *Education is vital, but many schools are overcrowded and under-resourced. Suggest some strategies to improve educational opportunity for students learning in these environments.*

3 *What can be done to reduce crime in today's world?*

4 *Studies show that those who get a good start in life do better as adults. How can we ensure that all children receive the care and attention they need to develop into responsible and fulfilled citizens?*

UNIT 5

Discussing advantages and disadvantages

In this unit you will practise writing essays discussing advantages and disadvantages. You will be focusing on contemporary issues and this will give you an opportunity to explore the implications of modern lifestyle choices. Your essays will present a fair and balanced view of topics, while still making clear your own views and opinions. Part 1 focuses on the advantages and disadvantages of television, advertising and shopping for luxury goods. Part 2 explores the advantages and disadvantages of computer-based leisure and modern life in urban areas.

PART 1 ADVANTAGES AND DISADVANTAGES – THE MEDIA, ADVERTISING AND SHOPPING

Activity 1 Planning an essay

1 Read this information about the evolution of television. Complete the final sentence in an appropriate way.

There is evidence that, in many parts of the world, leisure time has increased in recent decades. At the same time, there has been a rise in the ownership of televisions, with many families having more than one set. There has also been a growth in cable and satellite broadcasting, with a corresponding increase in the type and variety of programmes available. Consumers have come to expect that they will be able to find a TV programme to suit their personal preferences, at any time of day or night. The evolution of television has implications* for the way we live. For example, children may have their own TV sets in their bedrooms and …

*results or effects

2 Study this essay question and highlight the key words. What issue do you have to consider? Write down the key issue in your own words.

TV ownership has increased dramatically in many parts of the world. Although many people believe TV has many more benefits than drawbacks, there are others who think TV has had negative effects on our lives.

Discuss the advantages and disadvantages of the increase in TV ownership.

In the essay question, you have to discuss the advantages (good points) and disadvantages (bad points). In your conclusion, you will say whether the advantages are greater than the disadvantages.

Activity 2 Brainstorming ideas

1 You already know that the next step is to brainstorm your ideas. Divide a page into two columns and brainstorm the advantages and disadvantages of television. Do this before you read the brainstorm on the next page.

James has brainstormed these ideas for his essay on the advantages and disadvantages of television. Are any of your ideas here? Underline them.

Advantages	Disadvantages
Affordable home entertainment – cheaper than computer, games consoles, etc.	A lot of advertising on TV – negative influence of advertising
Educational	Some programmes are poor quality
Good for people who are often at home e.g. carers of babies, elderly people	Changes social habits of the family – talk and interact less
People can enjoy programmes together and discuss programmes	Programmes show violence and antisocial behaviour
Watch in safe home environment	
Cheaper and easier than going out for entertainment	

2 Add this idea to the table.

TV is a passive experience – it is more fulfilling to be active and do creative activities.

Activity 3   An essay on pros and cons

An essential structure for an essay discussing advantages and disadvantages is:

- Introduction – refer to the question and say that you will be comparing advantages and disadvantages.
- Main text – write at least one paragraph on advantages and one paragraph on disadvantages. For a longer essay write more paragraphs.
- Conclusion – sum up the advantages and disadvantages and say which one outweighs the other.

James has considered both the benefits of TV and its disadvantages, and he has decided that TV has more advantages than disadvantages.

Read James's main paragraphs about the advantages and disadvantages of the TV. How far do you agree with James's views? Do you think he gives a reasonably balanced view of the pros and cons of television? Choose the correct expression from the pairs in italics.

TV has many advantages for family life. In the first place, TV provides ordinary families with affordable entertainment they can enjoy at home. This makes life more pleasurable and is particularly helpful for those who cannot go out easily such as the elderly and those caring for babies. *Secondly,/Despite* TV is educational. People can increase their knowledge of a wide range of subjects, find out about new developments in science and technology and *namely/also* keep informed of world events. In addition, parents can use the knowledge gained from TV to help their children with homework. *Surely/Finally*, parents and children can watch an interesting programme together and enjoy a shared learning experience.

Nevertheless/Moreover, there are certainly *drawbacks/benefits* to TV ownership, especially with regard to the social habits of families. Instead of talking or playing a game together, individual family members may be watching different programmes in separate rooms. *As a result/As such,* there is less quality time together as a family. *A further concern is that/In contrast* TV programmes may transmit values and expectations which are against the moral code children have been brought up to follow. TV dramas, *however/for instance*, may show children being rude to their parents. *If/Whether* this is shown as socially acceptable, children who have been brought up differently may become confused. *In fact/Although* some children may be so influenced that they begin to copy the examples of disrespect they see on TV.

Activity 4   Writing an introduction

James's essay needs an introduction. In an advantages/disadvantages essay, the introduction should say clearly that you are going to consider both sides of the question in an objective and fair way.

Choose the correct introduction from these two introductions.

A The increase in TV ownership has brought enjoyment to many people. There are others, however, who are understandably very concerned about the negative influences of TV. In this essay, I am going to compare the advantages and disadvantages of the rise in TV ownership and its implications for family life.

B The increase in TV ownership has brought pleasure to many people. There are others, however, who are concerned about the effects of excessive TV watching. The TV undoubtedly plays a big role in our lives. In this essay, I am going to focus on the advantages of the rise in TV ownership in terms of the effect on family life.

Activity 5   Writing a conclusion

If you believe that the advantages of the topic outweigh the disadvantages, it is good to show that you are taking account of problems you discussed earlier. To do this you can use conditions like *but only if*, *as long as* and *provided that*. For example:

• *In conclusion, I believe the advantages of renewable energy sources outweigh the disadvantages, **as long as** the problems of unreliability are resolved.*

- *To sum up, the advantages of taking out a student loan to study are greater than the disadvantages, **but only if** a careful budget is followed.*
- *To conclude, the advantages of rapid urban growth outweigh the disadvantages, **provided that** public services are developed to support the changes.*

When the disadvantages are greater than the advantages, it's good to give a reason which strengthens the negative implications outlined earlier. Reasons can be introduced with *because* or *as*. For example:

- *In conclusion, the disadvantages of leaving school early outweigh the advantages **because of** the permanent effect it can have on career opportunities.*
- *To conclude, the disadvantages of allowing children to access online chat rooms without supervision are greater than the advantages, **as** children can be harmed by adults using false identities.*

1 Complete these sentences. Be careful how you use commas.

a To sum up, the advantages of nuclear power outweigh the disadvantages (safety checks/carry out/regularly.)

b To conclude, the expansion of the home entertainment industry outweighs the drawbacks (have censorship/protect morals/values.)

c The disadvantages of being self-employed outweigh the advantages (more risky/insecure/ way/earn/living.)

d The disadvantages of English becoming a world language are greater than the advantages (local languages suffer/people/lose interest/learn them.)

2 Complete this sentence with a sensible condition e.g. *but only if/as long as/provided that*.

To sum up, I think the advantages of going abroad to study outweigh the disadvantages,

_____ .

3 Complete this sentence with a sensible reason e.g. *because/as*.

In conclusion, I think the disadvantages of teenage marriage outweigh the advantages,

_____ .

Activity 6 Comparatives

Remember:

The comparative forms of most short adjectives are formed by adding *–er*:

- a *richer* experience
- a *closer* family.

With longer adjectives use *more* or *less* to form the comparative:

- *more* interesting
- *more* rewarding
- *less* costly
- *less* enjoyable.

Use *than* to compare two things:

It is cheaper/less costly *to buy a new TV set **than** to replace worn out components.*

You can also use *as … as* to compare two things:

Opera is not **as** popular **as** pop music.

When you are forming comparatives you need to take care with spelling, irregular forms and exceptions.

1 In the conclusion to his essay, James uses several comparatives to highlight ways in which TV could be used to improve family life. Underline the comparative expressions in his conclusion below.

> In conclusion, I believe the advantages of TV outweigh the disadvantages as long as the TV is used wisely. For example, parents could be more careful about the type of programmes children watch. They could also discuss moral issues raised on TV so children develop more understanding of their family's values. As a result, far from being harmed by TV, the family could become stronger and closer.

2 Make these sentences comparative using words from the box. We have done the first one for you.

flexible	thrilling	memorable
expensive	passive	aware
enthusiastic		

1 Entertaining friends with a DVD at home is _____ going to the cinema as you can pause the DVD when you need to hand around drinks and snacks.

Entertaining friends with a DVD at home is more **flexible** than *going to the cinema, as you can pause the DVD when you need to hand around drinks and snacks.*

2 A family visit to the ballet is _____ watching a DVD at home and may be a talking point in conversation between parents and children for many years.

3 Watching sports events on TV is not _____ being a spectator at the actual event because you cannot share the tension of the crowd in the same way.

4 Attendance at theatres is falling as a result of the increase in home entertainment. As a result, tickets have become _____ they used to be.

5 Society is becoming _____ as a result of the expansion in home entertainment and people are _____ about going out to see a play or concert.

6 People used to be _____ of the physical and emotional efforts made by live performers.

Activity 7 Linking expressions

You looked at using linking expressions in Unit 4.

Ming has written an essay exploring the advantages and disadvantages of choosing to study for a career in the creative arts.

Here is a paragraph building up the advantages. Add the linking words from the box to connect Ming's ideas smoothly.

For example,	Finally,	Moreover,	In the first place,

> _____ students find the courses inspirational and gain a wonderful opportunity to develop themselves as creative artists. _____ they learn how to evaluate arguments and to think independently. When they graduate, there is a wide range of careers open to them. _____ there is 'artistic' work in their specialisms and careers in the media, advertising and marketing. _____ even though the job market is competitive, many graduates find good employment and are extremely successful.

Activity 8   Planning an essay – advertising

1 Study this essay question about the advantages and disadvantages of advertising, highlight the key words and make sure you understand what is required.

Advertising techniques have become more sophisticated. There are many who think this change is a positive development, but others have expressed concern about the possible negative impact. Explore the benefits and drawbacks of advertising for the consumer.

2 As you have done before, divide the paper into two halves and brainstorm the pros and cons of advertising. Before you do this, cover up the brainstorm below. It is always important to develop your own ideas first.

This is Charlotte's brainstorm for the essay question. Are any of your ideas here?

Benefits	Drawbacks
More knowledge of available products	Advertisers prey on people's fears/ insecurities
Information given in ways everyone can understand	Can be difficult to identify facts about products
Adverts are creative/entertain people	Difficult to ignore advertising (e.g. on TV,
Helps consumer to make comparisons/ choose appropriate products	cinema, magazines, etc.)

3 Only one of these points is relevant. Add it to the correct column.

- Encourages people to spend too much and get into debt.
- Many companies test their products on small groups of consumers before setting an advertising budget.

Activity 9   Proofreading

1 Charlotte has decided that, on balance, advertising has more disadvantages than benefits. This is her first draft. It is good but there is one mistake in each complete sentence. Find it and correct it.

Advertising is now so pervasive that it is difficult to ignore it, whatever part of the word you live in. Advertising has had some positive affects but it also has negative implications for people. In this essay, I am going consider the influences of advertising to the consumer.

Advertising undoubtedly has many advantage for the consumer. It helps consumers to be more aware of the products that are available and there particular qualities. People are, therefore, in a better position to make decisions about what to buy and how much to spend, which is especially helpful if you live in a Rural area. For example, I live 50 miles from a town and find it more convenient to check the products advertised on the Internet to make sure they are what I wanting, than to travel all the way to the shops only to be disappointed.

Nevertheless, there is a number of drawbacks to advertising. The most serious problem is that advertising prays on people's fears and insecurities. For example, some advertising techniques aim to persuade us that a hair gel will it make us more popular and successful. Even very much confident people are vulnerable to this kind of influence. In fact, advertising techniques can be so subtle that we may be unconscious off their influence.

To summing up, I believe that the disadvantages of advertising outweigh the advantages because some adverts exploit people's insecurities. People which are lonely or sad will not feel more positive just because they have bought a shampoo. Advertisers they encourage false wants based on insecurity. As the product does not meat a true need, it cannot satisfy the real requirements of the consumer.

2 This sentence was removed from Charlotte's essay. Put a * to show where it should go.

It can make people buy things they do not really want, just to feel better about themselves.

How far do you agree with Charlotte's negative appraisal of the advertising industry? Is she being fair or is she rather biased?

Activity 10 Using verb forms

Read this account of the history of advertising and correct the mistakes in verb forms.

Up until about 100 years ago, advertising was unsophisticated and was mainly focus on providing information about products. People's shopping habits was rational. People would not, for example, buy a new coat until their old coat had wear out. However, revolutionary psychological research change this attitude. The research demonstrate that people were drove by their needs for respect, love and their sense of emotional worth. Sales people were train to make the connection between people's need to feel good and shopping. So customers were made, in subtle ways, to feel less important or less respected if they did not bought expensive products. At the same time, clever advertising techniques reinforce the message that buying prestigious goods make you more important. Advertising become a thriving industry which was further help by growing prosperity and the introduction of the credit card.

Activity 11 Writing paragraphs – shopping habits

Some people shop in ordinary shops and markets while others go luxury shopping in exclusive shops and designer boutiques. Each type of shop has different benefits. Where do you normally shop? What do you buy? Do you think you get good value where you shop? Would you ever go to a designer store and pay a lot of money for a special outfit?

1 You are going to write two paragraphs comparing the benefits and drawbacks of shopping for clothes in exclusive designer stores. Brainstorm your thoughts on the pros and cons, using vocabulary in the box to trigger some useful ideas.

top quality	exclusive	brand name	trained staff
valued customer	social status	budget-conscious	credit card
envious	luxurious	unique products	out of place
expensive	aspiration	prosperity	fashion trends
affordable	packaging	debt	prestigious
lifestyles	need	poor copies	wealth
desire	famous labels	value for money	downmarket
great bargains	investment	cheap offers	judgemental
			friendly

2 Use your brainstorm ideas to write your own paragraphs comparing and contrasting the advantages and disadvantages of shopping for clothes in exclusive designer stores. Each paragraph should be at least 75 words. Write carefully using good linking words, spelling and grammar.

Activity 12 Confusing words

Choose the correct word to complete each sentence.

1 The disease became *persuasive/pervasive* and eventually all parts of the body were affected.

2 Protecting his family and giving to charity were his most important *valuables/values*.

3 When all my purchases had been *done/made*, I took a taxi home.

4 His enemies knew he had a bad leg and devised ways to *exploit/express* this *vulnerability/sensitivity*.

5 The poet is famous for his ability to use nature *imagery/imaginary* in his verses.

6 Her new hair colour was so *subtle/secret* that most of her friends did not notice the change.

7 She was *unconscious/self-conscious* about the spot on her chin and hoped people were not looking at it.

8 Although the businessman tried to stay cheerful, at night his worries about money *preyed/prayed* on his mind.

9 Advertising encourages us to *aspire/inspire* to a lifestyle that many of us would love to have, even if we are not likely to achieve it.

Activity 13 Spelling

Here are some words which are often misspelled. Learn to spell them correctly using the 'look, say, cover, write' spelling method from Unit 2.

responsibly	happily	bigger	persuasive	pervasive

Activity 14 Academic style – tone and register

To create a more formal tone, suitable for an academic essay, avoid overusing the word *you* when it has a general meaning, and use a specific noun instead. For example:

You buy a particular kind of car so *you* can make others envious.

becomes

Motorists *buy a particular kind of car so **they** can make others envious.*

Replacing *you* with *motorists* and *they* makes the sentence more impersonal.

Replace *you* in the following sentences with a suitable noun (some of the letters of the replacement nouns are in brackets at the end of the sentence). Make any other changes necessary.

1 Discounts encourage you to spend more. (c _ _ _ _ _ _ s)

2 You need to wear proper swimwear at the swimming pool. (S _ _ _ _ e _ _)

3 You contribute to the local economy when you buy souvenirs on holiday. (T _ _ r _ _ _ _)

4 I believe you often feel anxious before undergoing an operation. (p _ _ _ _ _ _ _)

5 You enjoy the challenge of a competitive match. (Pl _ _ _ _ _)

6 You find it useful to have a revision schedule at exam time. (_tu _ _ _ _ _)

PART 2 ADVANTAGES AND DISADVANTAGES – USING COMPUTERS AND LIVING IN URBAN AREAS

Activity 15 Using computers in leisure time

 Many of us use computers at work or college. Computer use for fun and relaxation during leisure time is also rapidly increasing. Do you play computer games, have your own profile on a social networking site or take part in online games? What do you think are the benefits of computers? Are you worried about any adverse effects?

1 **Brainstorm some of the advantages and disadvantages of using computers for relaxation and social contact.**

2 **Now complete the following factual report about the effect of computer use on children's minds. Complete the gaps with a word from the box.**

habit-forming	doubled	actions	experts
attention	computer	mark	mindset

Neuroscientists say every experience leaves a _____ on the human brain. The effect of high levels of computer usage on the brain is unknown, but there are fears that it could affect our emotional development, be _____ and lead to shortened _____ spans. These effects are greatly increased by the expansion of computer use during our leisure time. Children, whose brains are still developing, are at most risk from high levels of usage. Perhaps because of parental fears about the safety of playing outdoors, the amount of time a child spends playing _____ games or chatting on online sites has _____ in the last three years. This has particular implications for children because they do not have the life experience to compensate for the new _____ they may be developing. Some _____ believe we may be bringing up a generation of children who fail to relate fully to others, concentrate properly or see the consequences of their _____.

Activity 16   Social networking sites

1 **Prakash has tackled this essay question. Highlight the key words and make sure you understand the question.**

Social networking sites are very popular in some countries. Clearly, many people enjoy talking to friends on the sites, but some experts warn that social networking sites could be harmful.

Compare and contrast the benefits and drawbacks of social networking sites for individuals.

2 **Read Prakash's essay and then decide whether these statements are true or false.**

1 The essay has a clear introduction, main part and conclusion.

2 There is a good standard of punctuation, grammar and spelling.

3 The essay is divided into logical paragraphs.

4 The advantages and disadvantages are compared well.

5 Prakash has answered the question set.

6 Prakash has stayed focused on the topic.

7 There is a good range of vocabulary used.

8 The style is suitable for an academic essay.

9 The conclusion takes account of the disadvantages outlined earlier in the essay.

In this essay, I will discuss the advantages of social networking sites, but also explore their drawbacks, particularly in terms of the implications for personal and social development.

There are many advantages of social networking sites. In the first place, groups of friends can stay in touch easily, without the expense or inconvenience of going out to meet. It is also possible to broaden your social life by making new friends and acquaintances. Building a personal profile on the sites gives users a sense of importance and increases self-esteem. Self-esteem is further helped by the fact that appearance or body language is irrelevant. In addition, the sites are accessible 24 hours a day, so the enjoyment and *reassurance* of social contact is constantly available. Overall, networking sites help meet the human need to belong, to have recognition and to be valued.

There are some drawbacks, however, to the sites. The qualities of patience and empathy which are required for friendships in the real world are less necessary in the cyber world. People who are communicating on networking sites, for example, may not be aware of how others are really feeling, as there are no visual *cues* to influence interaction. Moreover, if communication is not *stimulating* enough, some users choose to move on quickly. There have been concerns that cyber-based *interaction* will begin to affect our ability to understand other people and their emotions.

In conclusion, I believe, that the fun, flexibility and 24-hour access of the sites outweigh the disadvantages, but only if the time spent on them is reasonably limited. Social networking can never replace actual social contact. Users should meet friends regularly to ensure their *capacity* for real-life friendships continues to grow.

---

 3 **How far do you agree with Prakash's opinions? Do you think his views are balanced or not?**

4 **Match the words in italics in Prakash's essay to these words.**

signals	relating	comfort	exciting	ability

5 Indicate with a * where this example from Prakash's experience should go in the essay.

I used to lack confidence in new situations and as a user, it was comforting to know that these issues were of no importance.

Activity 17 Choosing the most relevant ideas

You may not use all the points from your brainstorm, especially as you learn to group ideas and think and plan in paragraphs. This was Prakash's brainstorm.

Put a * next to the points he chose not to include.

Keep in touch with friends
Make new friends
Build an identity on the site – makes you feel valued
Friendly 24-hour social contact
Do not need to be sensitive to body language
Less concern about how you might be evaluated
Good for shy people
Rapid interchange – constant stimulation
Cheap/saves time/expense/visiting friends
Instant feedback

Lack of empathy/understanding of real relationships
Real relationships more difficult to form
Could diminish quality of interaction in real life
Thoughts and feelings posted instantly, without reflection – reduces inhibitions/ sense of what is private
Conversations can be time-wasting
Encourages need for instant gratification
Can be addictive

Activity 18 Definitions

Match the sentences to the words in the box.

empathy	instant gratification	identity
body language	inhibition	online imagined societies
mindset		

1 This is something you have if you are able to appreciate how someone in distress is thinking and feeling.
2 A baby cannot understand the need for patience and demands this if she is hungry or miserable.
3 Someone who talks and acts freely, whatever the circumstances, does not have this.
4 Facial expression, mannerisms and ways of moving are all examples of this.
5 Millions of users have signed up for screen friendships on these.
6 Your name, family background, career, income level and the car you drive can all contribute to this.
7 Thoughts, mental attitudes and beliefs are all examples of this.

Activity 19 The challenges of urban life

1 Read this essay question and make sure you know what you have to do.

Many places which were once small towns have become big cities. This change may be slow or relatively fast. Explore the advantages and disadvantages of urban development.

These adjectives and expressions might be useful in your essay. Remember that if you use them for the comparative you need to add -er to short words e.g. *fast–faster* and *more* to longer words e.g. *more difficult.*

spacious	diverse	crowded	dull
polluted	noisy	dynamic	urban
stimulating	sprawling	anonymous	fast
challenging	interesting	pleasant	dirty
expensive	varied	surprising	lonely
unexpected	atmospheric	cosmopolitan	vital
(un)affordable	rural	urban	neighbourly
unemployed	peaceful	rapid	welcoming

Other useful expressions are listed below.

transport network	slum	town planning
overpopulated areas	new housing developments	local economy
level of demand	pace of life	traffic congestion
high living costs	quality of life	career opportunities
high-rise blocks	sense of community	health and education services
newcomers		

2 **Brainstorm the advantages and disadvantages of urban development.**

3 **Plan your essay following the steps below.**
- Select the relevant points from your brainstorm.
- Think and plan in paragraphs – one or two paragraphs for advantages and one or two paragraphs for disadvantages.
- Include an introduction and an evaluative conclusion.

4 **Draft the essay in rough first. Write at least 250 words.**

5 **Proofread your first draft for mistakes then produce a second draft.**

6 **Write another essay of at least 250 words on one or more of these titles.**

1 *Winning the lottery would be a dream come true for many people, yet a recent survey showed that nearly half the winners reported lower levels of happiness than before the win. Write an essay exploring the advantages and disadvantages of winning the lottery.*

2 *Young people are often advised not to marry until they have settled into a good career. Nevertheless, large numbers of young people still choose to marry before the age of 21. Explore the benefits and drawbacks of teenage marriage.*

3 *Write an essay exploring the benefits and implications of leaving home to study abroad.*

4 *More and more people are finding enjoyment in computer games, online games and online imagined societies. While some see no harm in this, others warn of the consequences it could have for society. Discuss the advantages and disadvantages of computer-based leisure.*

5 *Is it better to be self-employed and run your own business? Or is building a career in secure employment the better option? Discuss the advantages and disadvantages of self-employment.*

6 *Explore the effects of the Internet on family life.*

7 *Discuss the advantages and disadvantages of online auction sites.*

8 *What are the benefits and drawbacks of video sharing sites?*

9 *Many people now publish their views on the Internet through blogs, personal diaries and so on. Is personal online publishing a positive development? How do you feel about it?*

UNIT 6 Writing opinion essays

In this unit, you will explore how the media represent scientists and artists. You will also practise different ways of answering opinion essay questions. Some of these will be familiar from other units. Part 1 focuses on scientists and how they work and Part 2 explores art, money and stardom.

PART 1 WRITING ABOUT SCIENTISTS AND HOW THEY WORK

Activity 1   The role of scientists

Read the following extract from an article about scientists and how they work. Complete the final sentence of the second paragraph by choosing one of the options provided below.

> Scientific breakthroughs* are usually reported in the media as the work of a group of scientists. Scientists say that the collective nature of science is the key to its success. Shared values, for example, are more important than individual ambition or personality. 'We are just ordinary people who work hard to find things out' is a typical view.
>
> An international survey, however, showed that the public had a different view of scientists. Opinions ranged from 'inspired geniuses', to 'secretive', 'mad', and 'unethical'. As a result of the survey, a leading scientific institute decided to _____.

* discoveries

Options

  A *review its recruitment policy for scientists and change its selection criteria.*

  or

  B *create a public website showing the aims of projects and their progress.*

A stereotype is a fixed representation of what a group of people is like. For example, 'All teenagers are lazy and love pop music' or 'All grandmothers are homely and sweet' are stereotypes. A stereotype is often wrong because it does not show the complexity of the real person.

 How far do you think the media represent scientists in a stereotyped way?

Activity 2   Planning an opinion essay

1 Study this question and highlight the key words.

The media sometimes report that expensive scientific research has been a waste of money. What are your opinions of the research work scientists do? Are the benefits worth the expense?

What is the topic of the essay? What do you have to give opinions about? Is there an argument angle in the question?

You can answer this question by discussing the good and bad points of scientific research and considering the role of the media in reporting scientific research.

2 **Brainstorm your own opinions. What are the benefits of scientific research? What are the drawbacks? Divide a page into two columns for good and bad points. Cover up the brainstorm below before you start so that you work out your own ideas first.**

For example:

- benefits of research include vaccines against diseases
- drawbacks include unintended outcomes such as the nuclear bomb or the effects of the thalidomide drug.

Ayesha has organised ideas for and against scientific research into the lists below. Are any of her ideas similar to yours?

Introduction	
Benefits of research	**Drawbacks**
medical advances e.g. vaccines, transplants	some projects fail or there is no positive result
technological progress e.g. Internet, air travel, satellites, mobile phone	can lead to disasters/catastrophes e.g. nuclear bomb, thalidomide
increases knowledge or spin-offs in other areas e.g. space travel led to the development of home technological devices	research can be unethical – people and the environment may be badly affected by experimentation
Conclusion	

3 **Ayesha also thought of this idea. Add it to the correct column.**

Research priorities ignore urgent needs – luxuries are developed instead of essential things.

Activity 3 Reading and completing an essay

An essential structure for an opinion essay is:

- Introduction – refer to the question and say how you are going to answer it.
- Main text – write at least two paragraphs giving your opinions on the topic, with reasons and examples. You can also often evaluate an idea in an opinion essay, as Ayesha does.
- Conclusion – sum up your opinions clearly, reinforcing ideas you have mentioned earlier.

Ayesha's essay needs an introduction.

1 Choose the correct introduction from these two introductions.

A Scientists play an important role in modern life. In this essay, I am going to suggest that media reporting has had negative effects on the public's view of the validity of research and explain why, in my view, that is unacceptable.

B The work of scientists has had both good and negative effects on society. Currently, there is concern in the media that scientific developments are not used to benefit poor countries. I am going to question whether this concern has any basis in reality.

In her main text, Ayesha plans to answer the question by evaluating the idea that scientific research is not worth the costs.

2 Choose the correct expression from the pairs in italics.

In the first place, the media often focus on examples of failures in scientific research and ignore the many advantages we have gained. *Since/As I see it*, it is unfair to criticise scientific research for sometimes failing, because some trial and error is inevitable. *For instance/In addition,* the famous scientist Edison did thousands of experiments to find out how to make a light bulb work. This was not failure, *and/but* necessary experimentation, which eventually led to success.

Furthermore/Last but not least, sensational media reporting may aim to persuade us that scientists ignore urgent needs. Research efforts are directed towards the production of luxuries, not into essential improvements. *Although/For instance,* a recent media report criticised the expensive funding of a project to develop the best sort of potato for making potato crisps for the snack food market. *In my view,/While* scientists cannot control funding priorities or the applications of their work *so/but* it is unjust to blame them.

3 Read Ayesha's conclusion for sense and choose the correct word from each pair in italics.

To conclude, I believe the media *should/would* provide a more balanced view of scientific projects, and show that, while some projects *miss/fail*, the majority are *worthwhile/faultless*. Finally, without the work of scientists we would not have modern *benefits/technology*, including the Internet, vaccines, anaesthetics, or air travel. Thanks to scientists, life expectancy in the developed world is *twice/more* what it was a hundred years ago.

- How far do you agree with Ayesha's opinions?
- How far do you agree with Ayesha that scientists lack control in relation to research priorities and applications? Consider scientists' choices in who they work for.
- Would more media interviews with scientists help to overcome the stereotyped views the public may have?
- Few individual scientists become as well-known as famous people in the arts. On the whole, is this a good or a bad thing?

Activity 4   Supporting opinions with reasons and examples

Opinions are much more persuasive when they are supported with reasons and examples.
Examples are usually introduced with 'For example,' or 'For instance,'. For example:

As I see it, *it is unfair to criticise scientific research for sometimes failing,* **because** *some trial and error is inevitable.* **For instance***, the famous scientist Edison did thousands of experiments to find out how to make a light bulb work.*

1   **These sentences support opinions with reasons and examples. Underline the words used to introduce reasons and opinions. Then write out the examples in full. Note that a comma is sometimes needed before the word 'because' or 'as'.**

  a   I think it is pointless to believe everything the newspapers tell us, because the media often exaggerate. (recent newspaper reports claim/scientists/found gene/stop ageing/which/was/distortion/the truth.)

  b   It is wrong to claim that all scientists worry about moral principles, as not all scientists think about the ethics of what they do. (some scientists/continue/research/even if/there/possibility/projects/could do harm.)

  c   As I see it, it is ill-advised to stop learning about science at school, because the subject is important to modern life. (students might not find/job/if/do/not/understand scientific principles.)

  d   In my view, it is naive to follow all scientific advice without question, because scientific understanding may be superseded by new discoveries. (scientists believe/stomach ulcers/cause by/stress/but further research show/that bacteria cause/them.)

  e   It is questionable to fund research that only benefits a few people, as the nation's resources for funding are limited. (research/rare medical conditions/uses money/skills/could be better used/researching common diseases.)

  f   It is unjustifiable to stop research because some projects are expensive. (cancer research/costs/great deal money but/led to/much higher survival rates.)

  g   I believe it is immoral to carry out experiments on people without their permission, as some experiments can have harmful effects. (rich countries/be/criticised/unethical/research/done/poor countries.)

2   **Complete these sentences appropriately.**

  a   It is very limited to judge students' success on academic performance alone, because
      _____. For example, _____.

  b   As I see it, it is unwise to condemn all scientists because _____. For example,
      _____.

3   **Now write two examples of your own, following the pattern above.**

Activity 5   Confusing words

Choose the correct word or phrase in italics to complete each sentence.

  1   The report that he had been paid four million dollars for directing the project was *exaggerated/distorted*. He had, in fact, received less than one million.

  2   Children's TV uses *complex characters/stereotypes* to help young people identify quickly with the action and situation.

  3   With such high prices and poor-quality service, it was *inevitable/inefficient* that the restaurant would lose business.

  4   The company learned how to produce the perfect potato crisp, not by following a formula, but by *a trial period/trial and error*.

  5   It was understood that the new enterprise would not make a profit in the first year, but the management did manage to *break even/breakthrough*.

Activity 6   Using the correct vocabulary

1 The adjectives below are similar in meaning to the word 'wrong', except one word. Delete the word which is not similar in meaning to the word 'wrong'.

foolish	unwise	ill-advised	immoral
unjustifiable	faultless	pointless	invalid
worthless			

2 All the nouns in the box are used to say a person has reached a very high level in their field. Which word has the strongest meaning?

specialist	intellectual	expert	master
professor	genius	authority	mentor

Activity 7   Punctuation – the possessive apostrophe

For singular nouns, the possessive apostrophe is *before* the 's'. For example:

- the biologist's knowledge
- the student's teachers.

For plural nouns ending in 's', the possessive apostrophe is *after* the 's'. For example:

- the scientists' efforts
- the ladies' cloakroom.

The exceptions are *irregular plurals* where an apostrophe *is needed*. For example:

- the men's/women's/people's/children's charter.

It's with an apostrophe is short for *It is*.

An apostrophe is never needed in *its* in these examples:

- The company changed *its* recruitment policy.
- The snake shed *its* skin.

Similarly, an apostrophe is never needed in *yours*, *hers*, *theirs* or *his*.

An apostrophe is never needed in a plural where there is no possession. For example:

- Will you send her the books and DVDs?
- The breakthrough occurred in the early 1960s.

Add an apostrophe where necessary in these sentences.

1 Scientists autonomy is very important to them.

2 Is a physicists work just a job, or is it a vocation?

3 Engineers say that their work produces many benefits for the nations economy.

4 Even geniuses acknowledge their teams efforts. As the famous scientist Newton said, 'If I have seen a little further, it is by standing on the shoulders of giants.'

5 The project was presented at a conference for ministers. The ministers first reaction when the projects leader, Professor Kelly, explained the outcomes of the research, was one of unanimous disbelief.

6 The universities research staff spoke at a TV journalists convention to explain their latest breakthrough.

7 He was working as the research assistants administrator and frequently attended meetings on their behalf.

8   The photographs were stored on several CDs.

9   The government has asked its ministers to review the privacy laws.

Activity 8   Writing an opinion essay – the brain drain

Each year experts leave their countries for better job opportunities elsewhere. This is known as the 'brain drain'. In your opinion, is it right for experts to leave their home country? Does the country of origin ultimately benefit because the expert returns with more experience?

1   Brainstorm your ideas by dividing a page in two and writing down the points in favour of and against the brain drain.

2   Read the following essay question. Highlight the key words and make sure you understand what you have to do.

Experts sometimes leave their home country to take up new jobs abroad. Recent media reports suggested that this trend is likely to increase further. What are your opinions on this issue?

A straightforward way to answer this question is to evaluate the rights and wrongs of experts going overseas to work and say what your opinions are.

Here is an introductory paragraph for this question.

> The brain drain is a trend that affects many countries in the world. Each year, for instance, a large number of doctors and scientists leave Europe to develop their careers in Australia, Canada and the United States. In this essay I am going to discuss the rights and wrongs of the brain drain and why I am in favour of it.

3   Write at least two more evaluative paragraphs which would form the main part of this essay. Finally, add a conclusion which summarises and reinforces your earlier ideas. Your essay should be at least 250 words.

Remember to:

- brainstorm your ideas
- think and plan in paragraphs
- draft your essay in rough first
- proofread it for sense and for errors
- draft a final version incorporating your improvements.

PART 2 WRITING ABOUT ART, MONEY AND STARDOM

Activity 9   Writing about the creative arts

Have you ever noticed street artists painting pictures or street musicians playing instruments? Have you visited a market and seen handmade jewellery or clothing being sold by the designer? How much money would you give for work of this kind?

1   Many creative people are not rich or famous. What kind of contribution do creative people make to our lives? Are they paid fairly?

Discuss your ideas with others.

2 Study this essay question. Highlight the key words and make sure you understand what is required. Cover the completed brainstorm below before you start.

Many creative people producing artistic work are poorly paid and find it difficult to live on their earnings. Is this situation acceptable? What are your opinions?

This question could be answered with a problem-solving approach. For example, you could decide that it is wrong for creative people to earn low incomes and suggest strategies to help resolve this.

3 Brainstorm some strategies which would help solve the problem of low earnings for creative people. Cover the completed brainstorm below before you start.

Here is Li's brainstorm in answer to the question. Are any of your ideas here?

- educate people to understand why artistic work is worth paying good money for
- raise public awareness of the problem of low earnings in the creative arts
- encourage artists to join professional organisations/network with each other to share ideas
- increase penalties for illegal copying/downloading of music, films and so on
- universities, art colleges and music academies can advise students on how to negotiate fair rates
- organisations and individuals can promote the work of unknown artists through the media
- organisations and individuals can offer practical support such as buying original art or asking creative people to do workshops.

Activity 10   Proofreading

1 There is one extra word in each sentence of Li's essay. Proofread his essay and delete the extra word.

The media portrayal of creative people often gives the impression that these they are usually wealthy people. While it may be true that a few artists are rich, many do not make there a decent living, even though they are talented and produce original work. In this essay, I shall suggest some strategies to improve well the income of creative people.

In the first place, the public we could be educated more effectively about the value of an artist's work. If more people understood the effort that artists put into their work and the skills what they use, they would realise why they should pay reasonable prices. It may also deter people from buying illegal copies or downloading the music illegally.

A further solution is to encourage artists to join with professional associations. These associations can advise them how to market their work and what they should to charge for it. One of my favourite musicians, Sammy Worviel, was he almost cheated when he made his first record because he lacked business experience. Last but not least, artists could also be network with each other to build up commercial knowledge and social contacts.

2 Add the punctuation to Li's conclusion.

> in conclusion the good contribution creative people make to our lives means that they deserve a fair rate of pay i believe both the general public and official organisations could do more to protect artists from exploitation finally artists themselves need to learn better ways to produce and sell their work at rates that reflect its value

Activity 11   Academic style – avoiding contractions

Apart from possession, the apostrophe can show *contractions*. For example:

they are	they're
would have	would've
cannot	can't
is not	isn't
will not	won't
do not	don't

In academic writing, contractions should be avoided.

Read the following extract about stereotypes in the media and change the contracted forms to full forms.

> I've studied a range of characters portrayed in both film and TV dramas and I've concluded that they're often depicted in a stereotyped way. Although stereotyping gives us characters who are instantly recognisable, on the whole I believe it's detrimental to the audience identification with the character. When teenagers are stereotyped as 'lazy' or 'rebellious', the audience won't feel sympathetic to them or try to understand their motives. If we're to relate meaningfully to the characters, they should be more fully developed. Subtle, conflicting or complex elements of their personalities shouldn't be ignored or oversimplified. I think actors should challenge the director's control, if they feel they're asked to play a role inappropriately.

Activity 12   Spelling

1 **Here are some words which are often misspelled. Learn to spell them correctly using the 'look, say, cover, write' method from Unit 2.**

vaccine	scientist	technology	stereotype
exaggerate	distortion	inevitable	

2 **Now use two of these words in a sentence of your own.**

Activity 13   Writing an opinion essay about TV quiz shows

 Television quiz shows are a form of entertainment which has been popular with viewers for a long time. What makes quiz shows entertaining? Consider:

- jokes and humour
- the tense atmosphere
- the styles of the presenters
- the pressures on the contestants.

Would you rather be the contestant on a quiz show or the presenter? Try to explain your preference to a friend.

1 Now read the essay question and underline the key words. Make sure you know what is required.

TV quiz shows are a very popular and traditional form of entertainment. What do you think is the lasting attraction of the TV quiz show for the audience?

Should you answer this question by evaluating the rights and wrongs of quiz shows or by exploring your opinions on the question?

When an attraction lasts for a long time, it suggests that the audience is engaged by the entertainment at a deep level.

2 Brainstorm the following ideas about the techniques used to engage an audience in a television quiz show.
- Power relationships:
  - whether the presenters appear more powerful than the contestants.
- Identification:
  - whether we identify with the contestants or the presenter
  - how far we identify with the risk, opportunity and perhaps humiliation experienced by the contestants.
- Suspense:
  - whether the presenters do things to increase our suspense
  - whether the lighting, music, camera shots or seating help build up a tense atmosphere.
- Other techniques used to engage the audience and increase suspense.

3 Here is Kulwinder's answer to the question. Read it and decide whether the following statements are true or false.
a The essay answers the question.
b The essay is well organised.
c There is a good standard of punctuation, grammar and spelling.
d There is a good range of suitable vocabulary.
e The ideas are explained and developed.
f There is good use of reasons and examples.
g The style is suitable for an academic essay.
h The conclusion summarises the key points.

Television quiz programmes have continued to grow in popularity and appeal to audiences of all ages and social backgrounds. In this essay, I shall explore the importance of audience identification in giving this particular *genre* its *enduring* qualities.

In the first place, the presenter may act the part of a sympathetic uncle who tells us a little about the contestants' lives, emphasising in particular their struggles against misfortune. We are told, for example, if they have lost a parent at a young age, or never had the chance of a decent job. The more we are told about the *predicament* of the contestants, the more we identify with them and the more suspense we feel. If the contestants lose, we share their emotions of disappointment and even *humiliation*. If they win, we experience the thrill of their triumph.

Audience identification is also reinforced by the seating, the lighting and music. In the programme 'Make a Million' for example, the contestant sits alone on a low *stool* in the centre of a circle,

(continued)

waiting to be questioned. The seating suggests isolation and *vulnerability*. Winning could solve many of their difficulties. This *tantalising* combination of risk and opportunity keeps the audience breathlessly watching to the end.

To sum up, quiz programmes use several skilful devices to engage the audience and keep us on the edge of our seats. The relationship between the contestant and the powerful presenter is universally recognisable. Audience identification is so strong that, even if we are aware that our emotions are being *manipulated*, we are, nevertheless, happy to sit back and enjoy the show.

4 **Find words in italics which are similar in meaning to the words in the box.**

being in a difficult situation in life
a simple seat
exploited/being taken advantage of
something exciting we want very much though we may not get it
feelings of stupidity or shame
type of programme/artistic work
something that will last for a long time
weakness

5 **Answer these questions to show you understand Kulwinder's essay.**

   a How far do you agree with Kulwinder's views that audience identification and suspense are the key attractions of quiz shows?

   b How do you feel about the idea that there are universal aspects to the quiz show which we all identify with?

   c Do you agree that audiences' emotions are manipulated in quiz shows?

6 **Analyse the opinions in Kulwinder's essay by answering these questions.**

   a How far does Kulwinder's essay explore his own opinions on the question, rather than putting forward the rights and wrongs of quiz shows?

   b What devices has Kulwinder used to make his opinions persuasive? Consider the strength of his reasons and examples.

   c Consider the effect of omissions from the essay e.g. some viewers enjoy seeing others humiliated, many contestants work in strong teams, not alone.

7 **This is Kulwinder's brainstorm. Put a * against the points he chose not to include in his essay.**

Enduring attractions of quiz shows

   • prizes often extremely large
   • audience identifies with contestant – universal elements to their predicament
   • presenter may take role of severe judge – viewers enjoy seeing others humiliated
   • presenter encourages us to identify with the contestant
   • lots of humour/jokes

- suspense – use of dramatic music builds suspense
- sense of danger – dim lighting, music, isolation
- combination of risk and opportunity
- suspense – commercial breaks have delaying effects
- camera shots – close-ups increase suspense by showing strain on faces of contestants
- audience admires contestants' exceptional and expert knowledge.

Activity 14   Vocabulary check

Choose the correct word or phrase from the box to complete the sentences.

public image	enduring	aspire	identified
preserved his mystique	genre	universal	worshipped
represented	glorifies	publicity	

1   The idea of the young man from a poor home trying to find fame and fortune is a _____ idea which people from many different cultures will recognise.

2   The famous star _____ by rarely appearing in public or giving interviews to the media.

3   The television audience _____ more with the contestant when they were told that he came from the same town as they did.

4   Many people _____ to the rich lifestyles of famous people and would love to wear similar clothes or drive the same kinds of car.

5   His fans _____ the music star and refused to accept that he was just an ordinary person who had a good singing voice.

6   Talent shows have become a popular TV _____ and have led to previously unknown people becoming famous overnight.

7   Some people object to the increasing value of the prizes on quiz shows, saying it _____ money and materialism.

8   Although the famous actress was annoyed by the TV interviewer's questions, she answered politely as she did not want to damage her _____ .

9   Lack of _____ meant that many people did not even know the new film had been made.

10   Fans felt the star _____ their longings for a better, more fulfilled life.

11   His ability to create an instant rapport with the audience, even as he got older, gave the star his _____ quality.

Activity 15   What makes a star?

1   Think of some famous stars you know of – film stars, musicians, singers, dancers or footballers. Write down their names. What are the reasons why some individuals become 'stars' whereas others, although talented, never do?

2 **Brainstorm these aspects of being a star.**

- The skills and talents of the star.
- What the star represents to their fans e.g. freedom, an enviable lifestyle.
- Whether fans aspire to be like the star in some way.
- How the star relates to their fans.
- The role of the media in creating the star.
- Whether a previously unknown person can be made into a 'star' overnight.
- Whether the public image of the star has any relation to the reality of the real person.

3 **Read this essay question and underline the key words. What are the two things the question is asking for?**

What is the appeal of the 'star' for the audience? Is it possible for a 'star' to be made overnight? What are your views?

Does this question ask you to discuss the rights and wrongs of stardom, or for your opinions in general?

4 Now brainstorm your ideas on this essay question. The words in the box below may give you some ideas.

exceptional talent	unique	qualities
media representation	no one else like him/her	represents our hopes and dreams
glorify him/her	glitz and glamour	aspire to their lifestyle
special aura	preserve their mystique	never know who they really are
personal identification	admiration	feel a deep connection
worship the stars	compare ourselves with him/her	screen idols
public image	overnight sensation	blaze of publicity
talent shows	gossip magazines	fan clubs
catch the public imagination	be remembered	lack experience
disappear from public view	enduring qualities	soon forgotten
short-lived	vanish	passing fancy
stand the test of time	be discovered	

5 Plan and draft your essay. Write at least 250 words.

Remember to:

- select the best points from your brainstorm
- think and plan in paragraphs
- draft the essay in rough first
- proofread it for sense and for errors.

6 Write a final draft incorporating your improvements.

Activity 16 Writing an opinion essay – biased reporting

Have you ever noticed biased reporting (newspaper reports which use selected information to persuade the reader in an unfair or prejudiced way)? Which newspapers do you read? Are you happy that newspapers provide a balanced range of different views and opinions on an event or issue? Have you ever been concerned by factual inaccuracies?

1 Read the question below and underline the key words. What does the essay require?

In your opinion, how may a newspaper influence its readership?

2 Brainstorm your ideas.

Think about:

- omission of facts from an article
- choice of tone for an article (e.g. overcritical or excessively sympathetic)
- selection of strongly positive/negative pictures to accompany an article
- use of misleading information or statistics.

3 Read this report on the role of the newspaper editor and choose the correct words in italics to complete the text.

> Newspapers have traditionally played an important part *in/to* informing the public and influencing their opinions. The editor of *a/an* newspaper is particularly important because he or she selects the news reports. Editors also control the style and *tone/tune* of the newspaper.

(continued)

Editors take many factors *into/onto* account when choosing what to publish. One issue *is/are* the views of the owners of the newspaper. The amount of space available will also *effect/affect* news *coverage/covers*. Also very significant are the expectations of the target audience. Different newspapers *appeal/invite* to different target audiences. One kind of target audience, for instance, may expect *serious/grave* news. Another kind of target audience wants to be entertained. The editor selects celebrity *interviews/dialogue* and light-hearted stories to satisfy that need. *On the other hand/However*, all editors know that shocking or unusual news attracts attention, so the front page of any newspaper will focus on plane crashes, explosions, financial disasters and amazing escapes rather than *extraordinary/ordinary* events.

Readers sometimes complain *of/that* an event has been deliberately misrepresented or reported in a way which is only partly true. For example, important facts about a situation may have been left out, photographs accompanying the article may give an incorrect impression, or misleading statistics may be quoted. It is the responsibility *of/to* the editor to ensure that this kind of biased reporting is kept *in/under* control.

4 Brainstorm your ideas as usual, then plan the essay by selecting the key points from your brainstorm.

5 Make a rough draft, proofread it and then make a final draft incorporating your improvements. Write at least 250 words.

6 Write at least 250 words on one or more of these titles.

1 *How far do you think rich countries should share the results of their scientific research with poor countries? What are your opinions?*

2 *There is a proposal in your country to offer young people between the ages of 17 and 25 a free daily newspaper. How do you feel about this idea? What are your opinions?*

3 *A recent survey showed that parents advised their children to do a science or business course at university rather than an arts course. What are your opinions on this matter?*

4 *In some countries interest in studying a science subject at university is falling. Is there anything we could do about this issue or is it something we should accept?*

5 *Science is more advanced than ever. However, there is an increase in the numbers of people using alternative medicine that has not been proven scientifically. What are your opinions on this trend?*

6 *Choose one of the following groups and discuss how they are represented in the media:*
  * *the military*
  * *teenagers*
  * *families.*

7 *Choose one of these types of radio programme and explore its attraction for the audience:*
  * *talk shows*
  * *music programmes*
  * *phone-in programmes*
  * *current affairs programmes.*

8 *Should the media treat famous people differently from ordinary people? What are your views?*

9 *Some highly unusual news events generate a great deal of media attention. What influences might such media attention have on the way we feel about the world we live in?*

10 *Are 'stars' too influential in modern life? What are your opinions?*

11 *Television talent shows are becoming less entertaining. What are your opinions?*

UNIT 7 Describing visual information

In this unit you will learn to comment appropriately on visual information. In Part 1 you will describe graphs illustrating patterns in sales. Part 2 uses information about the natural world and the environment in the form of bar charts, pie charts and tables.

PART 1 DESCRIBING GRAPHS

Notes on using visual information

- When referring to visual information in writing, the word *figure* is used for all bar charts, line graphs, pie charts, maps and diagrams *except* tables. Tables are referred to as tables.
- Figures and tables should be numbered and given a title.
- In figures, the title is given below the data. In tables, the title is given above the data.
- Sources should be given for all data shown in figures and tables. (Some of the figures and tables in this unit are based on fictional information so no source is given for the data.)
- When commenting on visual information, pick out the most significant features on a chart or table to support your views. There is no need for very long descriptions, as visual information is designed to speak for itself.

Activity 1   Describing statistical change

1 Label Figures 1 to 5 with the appropriate description from this list.

a   A period of fluctuation followed by a slight increase.

b   A peak followed by a steep fall.

c   A gradual decline.

d   A dramatic fall followed by a period of no change.

e   A plateau followed by a steep/sharp increase.

2 Decide which of Figures 1 to 4 shows an upward trend and which shows a downward trend.

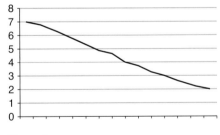

Figure 1

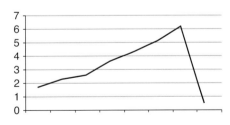

Figure 2

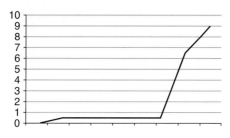

Figure 3

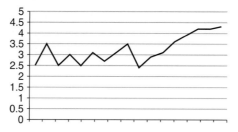

Figure 4

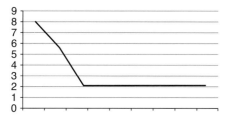

Figure 5

Figure 5 shows no change after the intial fall.

When there is little or no change, either up or down, we can say there is a:

- period of no/little change
- levelling
- plateau.

When there is a decrease or increase we can say:

- (There was/is) a considerable/significant/sharp/steep/dramatic/steady/gradual/ slight *fall/decline/decrease/drop.*
- (There was/is) a considerable/significant/sharp/steep/dramatic/steady/slight/ gradual *rise/increase/growth.*

or

- *X fell/declined/dropped* slightly/gradually/steadily/steeply/sharply/dramatically/ significantly/considerably.
- *X increased/grew/rose* slightly/steadily/gradually/steeply/sharply/dramatically/ significantly/considerably.

The highest point can be described in these ways:

- a peak
- X reached a peak
- X peaked at
- there was a peak at
- peaking at.

The opposite of a peak is:

- the lowest point/week/month, etc.

Trends can be described in these ways:

- an upward/downward trend
- the trend is up/down.

Activity 2 Comparing sales data from two companies

1 Study Figure 6 which shows the sales of two bicycle manufacturers, Speedrunner and Harry's Bikes.

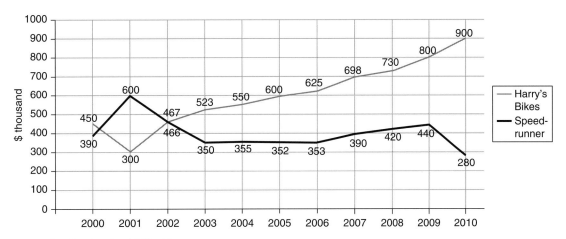

Figure 6 Bicycle sales 2000–10

2 Now answer these questions.

a What was the value of sales for Harry's Bikes in 2005?

b In which year did Harry's Bikes sales drop sharply?

c How much were the sales of Harry's Bikes worth in 2006?

d In which time period was there little change in sales for Speedrunner?

e Which company shows a steady upward trend in sales?

3 Complete this paragraph choosing the correct word from the pairs of words in italics.

The graph *show/shows* the bicycle sales for Harry's Bikes and Speedrunner between the years 2000 and 2010. Although sales fell *sharply/fast* for Harry's Bikes in 2001, the company has, overall, shown a steady upward trend in sales since 2002. In 2010, Harry's Bikes earned $900,000 from bicycle sales, an increase of 100% over 10 years. In contrast, sales for Speedrunner *peaked/risen* in 2001 with sales worth $600,000. Between 2001 and 2003, sales dropped *steeply/gradually* to $350,000. There was *little change/a drop* in the value of sales between 2003 and 2006. Although there was a *gradual/dramatic* rise in sales between 2006 and 2009, sales fell *gradually/significantly* in 2010 to less than $290,000.

4 Now write two more sentences about the graph.

Activity 3 Studying a sales graph

1 Study Figure 7 which shows the sales of two types of toiletries produced by a company called Greenlight. Then answer the questions.

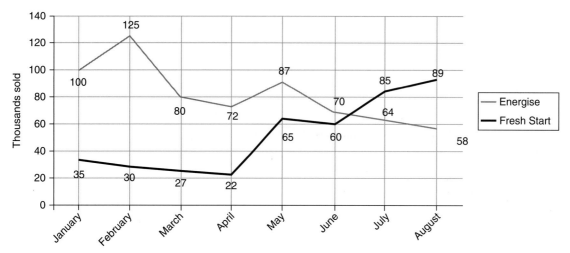

Figure 7 Volume sales Jan–Aug

a   Is the graph about income from sales or number sold?

b   What was the peak month for sales of Energise?

c   In which month did sales begin to show a gradual downward trend for Energise?

d   How much Fresh Start was sold in March?

e   In which month did sales begin to show a gradual upward trend for Fresh Start?

f   Which product had the better position in the marketplace in August?

2 Complete the paragraph with words from the box.

followed	change	down	illustrates	steeply
decline	contrast	peaking	fluctuation	

The graph _____ the volume sales of toiletries between January and August. There was a gradual _____ in Fresh Start sales between January and April. After this however, sales rose _____ and 65,000 products were sold in May. Between May and June there was little _____ in sales, but there was a gradual improvement between July and August.

In _____, sales of Energise rose significantly between January and February, _____ at 125,000 but this was _____ by a steep fall and period of _____. Between July and August, fewer than 65,000 products were sold each month. Overall, the trend for sales of Energise is _____.

3 Write two more sentences about Figure 7.

Activity 4 Describing a graph – toy sales

Figure 8 shows the sales of three international toy manufacturers – Funtime, PlayMe and Grow'n'learn. Write a paragraph of about 100 words describing the sales patterns of the three companies.

You might want to begin your paragraph like this:

Sales for …

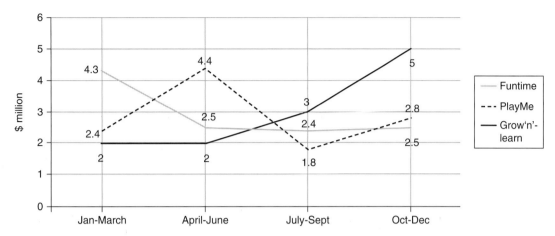

Figure 8 Toy sales Jan–Dec

PART 2 DESCRIBING BAR CHARTS, PIE CHARTS AND TABLES

Activity 5 Vocabulary check

The world's animal and plant species are classified in the following groups or classes:

- A Birds
- B Reptiles
- C Mammals
- D Fish
- E Plants
- F Invertebrates
- G Amphibians

1 Match the typical characteristics (1 to 7) below with the correct class (A to G) above.

1 Beak, feathers, no teeth.
2 Roots, seeds, photosynthesis.
3 Cold-blooded, scaly skin, eggs.
4 Warm-blooded, backbone, give birth to young.
5 Small size, no skeleton, no backbone.
6 Live in water, scales, fins.
7 Live on land and in water, often have limbs.

2 Now think of two or three examples of each class e.g. Birds: *eagle, swan*.

3 Some animals and plants in the world are at risk of becoming extinct (disappearing forever). Brainstorm some ideas about why you think this is and what could be done to stop it.

Activity 6   Writing about a bar chart – threatened species

1 Figure 9 shows the percentage of the world's species threatened with extinction. Study Figure 9. Then answer the questions.

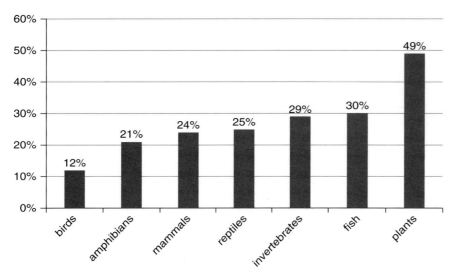

Figure 9   Percentage of species classified as threatened according to the International Union for the Conservation of Nature (IUCN), 2000

   a   What does the bar chart compare?

   b   What do the figures on the vertical axis (going up the left-hand side) represent?

   c   Which is the most threatened group, and which the least?

   d   Which groups are most similar in terms of threat experienced?

2 Complete the paragraph below using the approximations from the box. Some words need a capital letter.

nearly a third	ten per cent	one in five	about a quarter	about half

Figure 9 shows that _____ of the world's plant species are threatened, making them the most endangered group in the world. _____ of the world's fish and invertebrate species are at risk and _____ of the planet's mammal species. More than _____ of the planet's amphibian species are in danger. Birds are the least threatened group but, even so, more than _____ of this group are at risk.

3 Write a sentence of your own based on Figure 9.

Activity 7   Studying a table – animal populations

1 Table 1 shows estimated numbers of selected animals (mammals) alive in 2000 compared with the number alive in 1900. Answer these questions.

a   Which time period is covered in the table?

b   Is the area of the world where the animals live shown in the table?

c   Is the fall in numbers slight or dramatic?

d   In the table, which was the smallest animal population alive in 2000, and which the largest?

e   Would it be fair to say that, according to the table, the animals shown were coming close to extinction in 2000?

Table 1   Changes in world animal populations

Animal	1900 estimated population	2000 estimated population
Giant panda	65,000	650
Blue whale	335,000	4,500
Black rhino	1,000,000	2,000
Mountain gorilla	85,000	500

2 Complete the paragraph about Table 1 using words from the box. Some words need a capital letter.

compared	according	near	population
only	significantly	fell	

_____ to Table 1, only 650 giant pandas were alive in 2000 _____ with 65,000 in 1900. The numbers of the blue whale also _____ dramatically from 335,000 to 4,500. The _____ of the black rhino decreased _____ from 1,000,000 to 2,000. Finally, the mountain gorilla was also _____ to extinction, as _____ 500 were left alive in 2000.

3 If you could save one of these groups of animals from extinction, which would it be and why?

Activity 8   Analysing a table – endangered species

1 Table 2 shows that in some areas of the world the populations of certain endangered species has increased. Study the table. Then answer the questions.

Table 2   Changes in populations of endangered species

Southern white rhino, Natal, South Africa	Before 1980 – believed to be extinct	Current population in Natal – 11,000
Golden tamarin monkey (Brazilian monkey), Atlantic Coastal Forest, Brazil	Before 1970 – believed to be extinct	Current population in Atlantic Coastal Forest, Brazil – 12,000
Elephant, Kruger National Park, South Africa	In 1989 – 7,468	In 1995 – 8,371

a   Which rare species are mentioned in the table and where do these animals live?

b   How many years has it taken for numbers of each species to increase?

c   Which species has increased most significantly?

d   What do you think has helped preserve these rare species?

e   Write two sentences of your own comparing information in the table.

2   Theo has applied his skills in interpreting data in an essay about ways to protect endangered species. Read this extract and choose the correct word from the pairs in italics.

The *tables/diagrams depict/deploy* the rapidly *eliminating/diminishing* numbers of many rare species. It is clear that the giant panda, the mountain gorilla, the blue whale and the white rhino were *thriving/growing* in their respective *habitats/dens* one hundred years ago, but now these animals are almost *extinct/instinct*. For example, there is only a *handful/pocketful* of mountain gorillas left – 500 compared with 85,000 at the *turn/twist* of the twentieth century.

However, national governments and international agencies are working together to preserve rare species and have achieved some *notable/acceptable* successes. Kruger National Park in South Africa has implemented a successful conservation programme. As can be seen from Table 2, in the six years *of/from* 1989 to 1995, the population of elephants *has increased/much more* from 7,468 to 8,371. The *presence/presents* of park rangers also helps to protect animals and deters *killers/poachers*. *In addition/However*, Table 2 shows that the white rhino population in Natal, South Africa, which in 1980 was believed to be extinct, has *rose/risen* to 11,000 in 30 years. This has been achieved through *a combination/a variety* of moving the animals to protected areas and allowing some sport and hunting. *Finally/Surely*, the golden tamarin monkey has also benefited enormously through conservation and *captive/prisoner* breeding programmes. Before 1970, experts *knew/assumed* they were extinct but 12,000 of them now thrive in their natural *habitat/ nests* in Brazil.

Activity 9   Studying a pie chart – land use in South Africa

Variety in the Earth's environment is essential for biodiversity. Forest environments, grasslands, wetlands, deserts, polar regions and mountainous areas are all necessary if we are to maintain the diversity of our animal and plant species.

1   Study Figure 10 which shows types of habitat/land use in South Africa and decide whether the statements are true or false. If you think a statement is false, correct it.

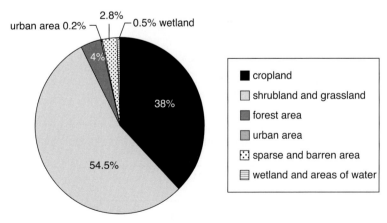

Figure 10   Habitat and land use in South Africa

a   Over half the land area is shrubland and grassland.

b   Forest areas make up 5% of the total land area.

c   Wetlands, areas of water and urban areas constitute more than 2% of the total land area.

d   Croplands are the next biggest land area after forest areas.

e   Sparse and barren areas make up 2.8% of the total.

f   Shrubland and grassland constitute a bigger area than all the other areas added together.

2 **Now complete this paragraph about the information in Figure 10 using the words in the box.**

the most dominant feature	according to	much less
comprises	total	largest

_____ Figure 10, over half of the total land area is shrubland and grassland. Croplands are the next _____ area and make up 38% of the total. Areas designated as sparse and barren form 2.8% of the total area. Wetlands and land for urban use are _____ significant and constitute less than 1% of the _____ land area. Shrubland and grassland is clearly _____ and _____ more of the total land area than all the other types of land put together.

3 **Now write a sentence of your own about the forest areas in Figure 10 and indicate where the sentence could go in the completed paragraph in question 2.**

Activity 10   Studying a pie chart – land use in Asia

1 **Study Figure 11 which shows habitats and land use in Asia. Then answer the questions.**

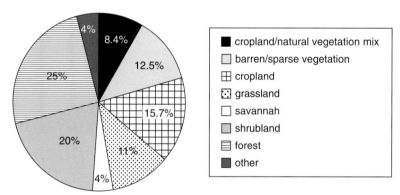

Figure 11   Habitat and land use in Asia

a   Which habitat constitutes a quarter of the total land area in Asia?

b   Which type of habitat/land use comprises one-fifth of the total land area?

c   Which is the third biggest type of habitat or land shown in Figure 11?

d   Which are the two smallest types of land or habitats shown in Figure 11?

2 Now write a short paragraph of about 80 words based on **Figure 11** commenting on habitat and land use in Asia.

You may find the words and expressions in the box helpful.

make(s) up	constitute(s)	account(s) for	comprise(s)

You can begin:

According to Figure 11, …

3 Alexi has applied the skills of interpreting data in discussing the importance of the natural habitat, based on **Figures 10 and 11**. Complete the paragraphs from his essay by choosing the best word or expression from the box.

temperate	as a result	poignant
fallen	eroded	thorny
candles	reduction	recent
suburbs		

As we can see from Figure 10, over half of South Africa is shrubland and grassland. This is a vital habitat for many rare species but these areas are gradually being _____ by sprawling _____, factories and farming. Consequently, the habitat for insects, birds and mammals is under pressure; for example, giraffes eat the _____ plants that grow in these grassy habitats so they are moving further afield in search of food.

In Asia, forested areas, as depicted in Figure 11, account for a quarter of the total land area. Today, the forests of Asia, both tropical and _____, are being cleared. One of the most _____ examples of the effects of forest clearance is the _____ in the number of orang-utans which live among the palm trees of the Indonesian rainforest. Soap, food and _____ are all valuable products of the palm trees. About 1.8 million hectares of rainforest, which includes many palm trees, are being destroyed every year for commercial reasons. _____ of habitat destruction, the number of orang-utans has _____ from 230,000 to only 60,000 in _____ years.

Activity 11   Studying a bar chart – ecological footprints

 Resourcing each person's lifestyle has a cost to the environment. This is sometimes called an 'ecological footprint'. Which countries do you think have a big ecological footprint, and which a small one?

1 Study **Figure 12** on the next page which shows the ecological footprint of each individual in selected areas of the world. Then answer the questions.

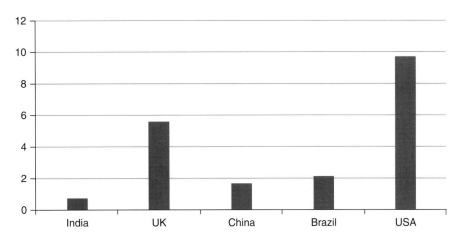

Figure 12 Hectares of productive land or sea needed to resource the lifestyle of one person, 2002

a   How is an 'ecological footprint' measured, according to Figure 12?

b   What do the bars in Figure 12 compare?

c   What do the numbers on the vertical axis represent?

d   Does Figure 12 show all countries or only selected areas of the world?

e   Which two countries on the chart have the most significant ecological footprint?

f   Which country on the chart has the least significant ecological footprint?

g   Is it fair to say that there is a large difference between the selected countries, in terms of their ecological footprint?

2   When comparing the ecological footprints of different countries, Theo wanted to emphasise the big differences that exist. Complete the paragraph with words and expressions from the box.

far more	even one	consumes only	under
next largest	by far the biggest	illustrates	

Figure 12 _____ the hectares of land or sea required to resource the lifestyle of one inhabitant from selected countries. It is clear from the chart that people in richer and more developed areas of the world consume _____ resources than those in less developed countries. The USA is _____ consumer of resources per head of population. For example, an individual in the USA uses almost ten hectares whereas an individual in India does not consume _____ hectare. China _____ 1.6 hectares per head of population – _____ six times less than the USA. At 5.6 hectares per person, the UK is the _____ consumer of resources shown on the chart after the USA.

3   Now write two more sentences about Figure 12.

Activity 12 Analysing a bar chart – CO_2 emissions

1 Study Figure 13. Then answer the questions.

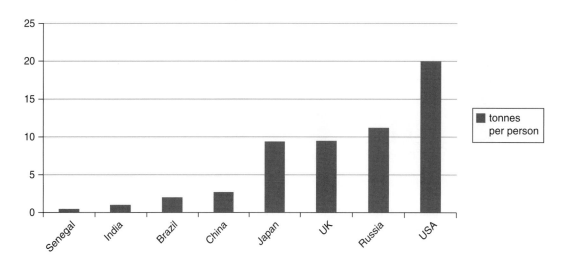

Figure 13 CO_2 emissions from the burning of oil, natural gas and coal, 2003

   a   What do the bars in Figure 13 compare?

   b   What do the figures on the vertical axis represent?

   c   Which two countries shown on the chart produce similar levels of emissions?

   d   Can we tell from Figure 13 that the USA is the biggest producer of emissions in the world?

2 Complete the paragraph using words and expressions from the box.

by far	yearly	more than double
great	eight	less developed

Figure 13 compares the _____ emissions of carbon dioxide from a selection of countries. There is clearly a _____ difference in levels of emissions between richer and _____ countries. Of the _____ countries depicted on the chart, the largest producer of CO_2 _____ is the USA which produces 20 tonnes per person of carbon dioxide emissions each year. This is _____ the amount produced by the UK or Japan.

3 Write three more sentences about Figure 13 comparing emissions between countries.

Activity 13 Urban growth

By the end of 2010 half the population of the world (3.3 billion) was expected to be living in urban areas and towns. Growth in urban population is known as urbanisation and this trend is expected to continue.

1 Without looking at Figures 14 and 15, think about these questions.

   a   Why do you think people want to move from rural areas? Consider opportunities in cities, lifestyles and employment prospects.

   b   What do people require in cities in order to live comfortably and safely?

   c   How can people benefit the cities they live in? Consider the qualities and skills they bring with them.

   d   Do you think rich and poor areas of the world will have similar levels of urbanisation? If you think there will be a difference, explain why.

2 Study Figures 14 and 15 and decide whether the statements are accurate or inaccurate. If you think a statement is incorrect, change it to make it accurate.

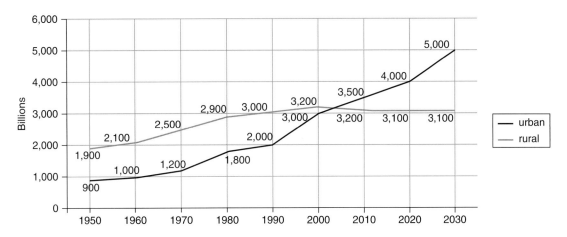

Figure 14 Global urban and rural population projections, 1950–2030

Which of these statements are accurate? Figure 14 shows that:

a In 1950, the global urban population was bigger than the rural population.

b Between 1950 and 1990, the urban and rural populations grew at a fairly similar rate.

c After 1990, there was a rapid increase in the size of the world's urban population

d After 1990, the global urban population began to level out while the rural population increased dramatically.

e By 2030, there will be no significant gap between the size of the urban and rural populations in the world.

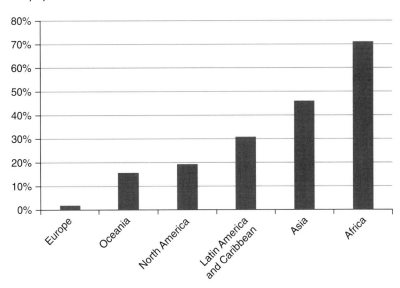

Figure 15 Projected percentage increase in urban populations, 2000–2015

Which of these statements are accurate? Figure 15 shows that:

a Urban populations are expected to increase by 2015.

b The urban population of Asia is predicted to increase more than in any other part of the world.

c The urban population of Oceania (islands of the central and South Pacific including Australasia) will have a bigger percentage increase than North America.

Now write two paragraphs summarising the trends shown in Figures 14 and 15.

3 Hannah has written an essay exploring the challenges of urbanisation. Read the first two paragraphs of her essay and choose the best word from the words in italics.

In the first paragraph, Hannah describes the data in the chart.

> According to Figure 14, the trend towards urbanisation, which began in 1970, has grown *steadily/easily*. By 2000, the urban population of the world *seeded/exceeded* those living in rural areas for the first time. It is projected that, if this *habit/trend* continues, by 2030, most of the world's population, 5 billion people, will be living in urban areas. Other recent data (Figure 15) show that urbanisation will be particularly *marked/pressured* on the continent of Africa where the urban population is *told/predicted* to increase by 70%. Urbanisation will also have a big *impact/damage* in Asia where the urban population will grow by 45%. Europe will be least *affected/effected* by the trend towards urbanisation with a projected *rise/risen* of about 1%.

Note that in these paragraphs, Hannah gives her own opinions.

> Although it is claimed by some authorities that urbanisation will lead to *squalor/discomfort*, poverty, overcrowding and rising crime *layers/levels*, I believe urban growth can be positive. In the first place, it is young people *who/which* are most likely to move from rural areas to cities and they bring with them *pessimism/optimism* and a strong motivation for a better life. For example, *newcomers/strangers* from rural areas have had a powerful impact on some modern cities, making them much more important.
>
> As I see it, the key issue for successful urbanisation is efficient management of land and resources. For example, Singapore is now 100% urbanised but it was recently *named/given* as one of the world's most attractive places to live. The land use is excellent and includes many beautiful parks. It also *has/have* good infrastructure. As long as opportunities *exist/offer*, places which are insignificant now could become *vibrant/vibrate* cities with strong economies and a well-developed infrastructure.

Activity 14   Further practice

1 Look back at Activities 9 and 10 about land use. Find out the breakdown of land use in your own country or a country which interests you. Write a short report on the land use in that country and present it to your class.

2 Choose a topic that interests you. Research it carefully and find some bar charts, pie charts or line graphs to illustrate it. Write your project up or present it as a talk, using the visual information to make it more interesting. When you present your talk, engage your audience by highlighting the most interesting features of the data.

3 You may also like to review projects that you are preparing for your other subjects. Try to find some stimulating visual data to illustrate your project and make brief comments on what the data show.

LANGUAGE BANK

This Language bank provides a range of useful expressions for describing visual information. Most of the expressions come from this unit.

Expressing change

You can use adjective + verb expressions to express change.

There is/was …

When there is *little change* we can say:

little/slight/no change little difference between	a levelling no significant difference/gap	a plateau*

* a high, level period of stability

When there is *significant change* we can say:

considerable steep	significant dramatic	marked steady	sharp

For a change *downwards* we can say:

fall	decline	decrease	drop

For a change *upwards* we can say:

rise	increase	growth

Or you can use verb + adverb expressions to express change.

The number …

fell/declined dropped/decreased increased/grew/rose	+	slightly/gradually steadily/steeply sharply/dramatically significantly/considerably

The highest point can be described in these ways:

a peak there was a peak at	reached a peak peaking at	peaked at

The opposite of a peak is:

the lowest point/week/month

Trends can be described in these ways:

an upward/downward trend the trend is up/down

Fluctuation can be described in these ways:

> there was a period of fluctuation
> fluctuated

Approximations

nearly a third	approximately ten per cent	one in five
about a quarter	about half	almost double
six times less	under/over	approximately one eighth
the majority	approximately three-fifths	

Comparisons

compared with	less than	more than
more important	less important	larger
smaller	least	most
largest	smallest	next largest
most significant	most dominant	similar
the same		

Time expressions

by 2015	by the end of 2010	in 1970
1950–90	between 1950 and 1990	before/after 1990
for three months	since 1900	during March
during the period 2010–30	fifty years ago	in the 1950s

Comprising

accounting for	comprise(s)	make(s) up	constitute(s)	account(s) for

Introductory expressions

> The graph/diagram/table shows/illustrates/indicates/depicts
> According to Figure 4,
> Figure 15 compares

Generalising

> In general,
> Overall,
> As a whole,

This unit is about writing personal statements and CVs. In Part 1 you will learn how to write a personal statement for university entrance. In Part 2 you will learn how to write a good CV and covering letter of application.

PART 1 WRITING A PERSONAL STATEMENT

Activity 1 Reasons for applying for a university course

 1 **What are your reasons for applying to university? Brainstorm some ideas on paper (rough notes are fine). Keep all your ideas as you will find them very useful later.**

2 Read these examples of reasons students give for applying for a course.

Marie's reason for applying to university is good because it shows interest in the subject:

Studying marketing will help me understand how the economy changes to reflect the changing needs of society.

But Chan's reason is not appropriate because it does not show interest in or knowledge of the subject:

I want to apply for marketing because I have not studied it before and so I do not know much about it yet.

3 Three of these reasons for applying to university are appropriate. Which reason is inappropriate?

I am applying for this degree because:

  a It offers the combination of intellectual challenge and the opportunity for a rewarding career.

  b I can achieve a well-paid career after graduating without needing top grades.

  c I will be able to acquire knowledge in an exciting, rapidly advancing field.

  d It gives me the opportunity to study the subject at the cutting edge.

Activity 2   Explaining why you are interested in a subject

1 *Because* and *as* are used to show reason. For example:

*I am applying to study economics **because** I find it a fascinating and challenging subject.*

Create sentences using *because* or *as* from these prompts.

  a applying this subject/love analysing character/motivation

  b want to do this degree/can arrange the course/suit my particular academic interests

  c interested/this subject/offers the opportunity/integrate/fascination/science with/desire/help people

  d applying this degree/opportunity/develop/critical thinking/analysis skills

2 *Furthermore, in addition* and *moreover* are used to add more reasons. For example:

In addition, *the course offers exciting work experience in international banking.*

Furthermore, *I will be taught by highly respected experts in a world-class environment.*

Moreover, *the course offers unique opportunities for scientific fieldwork overseas.*

Write an additional reason to follow each of these sentences. Use the prompts in brackets and one of the expressions above. Use a comma after each expression.

  a I am applying for this course because of the variety of modules I can choose from. (second term allows/particular focus/one topic area)

  b I am interested in this subject as I want to learn how to diagnose and treat disease. (practical experience in clinical setting)

  c I am applying to this university department because it has an excellent reputation for developing research skills. (multilingual and varied academic programme)

  d I am applying for this subject as it will enable me to develop skills in research, communication and analysis. (develop fluency in a European language)

3 Make a draft of your own reasons for going to university using *because/as* and *in addition/ moreover/furthermore*. Use your rough notes from Activity 1 and add any other ideas.

4 Read what you have written. Have you done yourself justice? Improve what you have written if you think you need to.

Activity 3   Explaining how long you have been interested in a subject

The *present perfect* + *since* or *for* can be used to show how long you have been interested in a subject. *Since* is used for a point in time in the past whereas *for* is used for a period of time. For example:

*I have been interested in the solar system **since** I was a small child.*

*I have been interested in business ethics **for** the last three years.*

The *present perfect continuous* is used for an activity which began in the past and is still continuing. For example:

I have been reading *about social policy since I was 14.*

I have been learning *Spanish for two years.*

1 **Add *since* or *for* to the gaps in these sentences.**

    a   I have been fascinated by banking _____ the sixth form.

    b   I have been curious about this subject _____ several years.

    c   I have been enthusiastic about studying this subject _____ I did a work placement in a clinic.

    d   I have been improving my knowledge of international relations _____ nine months.

    e   I have been researching the political and cultural influences on Malaysia _____ last summer.

    f   I have been practising my language skills _____ two years.

2 **Write a true sentence about your studies using *since* or *for*.**

University tutors will be most intrigued to know what triggered your initial enthusiasm in the subject you have decided to study in depth. This will be different for each person.

You can use the *present perfect + since + when* to say what started your interest in the subject. For example:

I have been fascinated *by banking* **since** *the sixth form* **when** *we did a project analysing international trading patterns.*

I have been researching *the political and cultural influences on Malaysia* **since** *last January* **when** *I visited the country on a family holiday.*

3 **Match the two halves of these sentences.**

    a   I have been learning about the history of China since I was 17 …

    b   I have been curious about nutritional chemistry since I was 15 …

    c   I have been developing my computer skills since my IGCSE year …

    d   I have been interested in physics since I was 11 …

    e   I have been curious about electricity since I was nine …

    f   I have been interested in speech therapy since starting secondary school …

    i   … when I helped my father repair my mother's hairdryer.

    ii   … when I made friends with a child who had a stammer.

    iii   … when my twin sister was diagnosed with diabetes.

    iv   … when I did a school project on music transmission.

    v   … when I worked in Beijing on a 'gap year' project.

    vi   … when we built a website as part of an IT project.

4 **Write a sentence explaining the reason using the words and phrases in the box.**

fascinated	space science	my seventh birthday
I	given	telescope

5 Think about what started your own interest in the subject you want to do. Any relevant reason will be valid, no matter how offbeat or unusual it is. Then use your ideas to complete this sentence.

I _____ _____ interested in _____ since _____ _____ when _____.

There may be other ideas you want to add about what triggered your interest in your subject. If so, write some more sentences.

Activity 4   Writing about your reading

University tutors are very curious about the reading you have done around your subject, especially any 'wider' reading. This could include reading from a variety of sources including magazines, journals, and information on the Internet.

1 Brainstorm some ideas about any wider subject reading you have done and why you have enjoyed it.

2 Here is an extract from Tanya's personal statement. What wider reading has she done and what has she learned from it?

> At school, we have been studying the work of Jane Austen for A level. In addition to the set texts, *Persuasion* and *Mansfield Park*, I have read three other novels by Jane Austen and two biographies. From my reading I have learned more about the theme of personal maturity and the importance of humility in the individual.

3 Now write these sentences in full using the words in brackets.

a   Since (start) pre-university course, I (be) (learn) about the impact of industrial change on society. In addition to the prescribed course reading, I (be) downloading business articles from the Internet. From my reading, I (learn) more about the way companies respond to changes in the market.

b   For the last two years, I be (interested) in the work of Polanski. In addition, to (study) his films in class, I (be) (research) articles about Polanski on the Internet. Recently, I (be) (read) critiques of his work in journals such as *Contemporary European Cinema*. From my (read), I (be) (learn) more about the influence of Polish history on Polanski's work.

4 Draft some complete sentences about the reading you have done and what you gained from it.

5 Read this paragraph from a personal statement and choose the correct word or phrase from the pairs in italics.

> *I was interested/have been interested* in Oriental Studies *since/for* I was 13 *where/when* we had an exchange teacher from Japan at our school *for/since* one year. She *has taught/taught* us to speak Japanese and *has introduced/introduced* us to novels by Japanese authors. I particularly like the novels by An Kazuki and can read them in Japanese with the help of a dictionary.
> The novels are set in the past and show how historical events *have shaped/shape* modern Japan and made the country what it is today. *In addition/However*, I listen to a Japanese news broadcast each day which has developed my knowledge of vocabulary and key political figures in contemporary Japan.

Activity 5 Explaining your reasons

1 Now use your notes from Activity 1 to draft two complete paragraphs explaining why you want to do your chosen subject at university. Write about 75 to 100 words for each paragraph.

Before you start writing, plan what you are going to write using this list.

- Give clear reasons for your application.
- Say how long you have been interested in the subject.
- Say what started your interest in the subject.
- Say what you have read about the subject.
- Say what you have learned from your reading.
- Add any other ideas of your own.

2 After you have written your first draft, check it carefully. Does what you have written accurately reflect the high level of your potential and skills? Make any improvements and write your final draft.

3 Proofread your final draft and correct any errors. Show your final draft to a friend and ask for feedback. Do their ideas better reflect the 'real' you? Write a last version, incorporating any changes.

Activity 6 Your leisure time

As you know, being an effective student is not only about studying. Keeping physically fit is enjoyable in itself, and it helps you to be more mentally alert. Being able to relate comfortably to others will also benefit you at university. Showing that you have these skills is important for your personal statement as they are evidence of a balanced approach to life. So, in your personal statement, you need to make the link between how you enjoy yourself in your leisure time and the course you want to do, or university experience in general.

1 Make a note of how you have fun and what you get out of it.

Here is an example.

I play in a band in my free time. I enjoy it and it has helped me rise to new challenges.

Starting sentences with 'I' means that what you write is clear and understandable. However, it is good to vary the style of your sentences, so they don't all start with 'I'. To do this, some sentences can start with a present participle (*-ing* form). For example, compare these two sentences.

I play tennis in my free time. It's sociable and the exercise helps me relax.

Playing tennis in my free time is sociable and the exercise helps me relax.

The second sentence has a more varied structure which will improve the overall style of your writing.

2 Join these sentences together, starting with a present participle.

   a I visit art galleries. This is eye-opening and inspires me to be more adventurous in my own artwork.

   b I watch foreign films. It has given me insights into other cultures.

   c I make my own clothes. It's creative and cheap.

3 Write a similar sentence about your own leisure interests, starting with a present participle.

Activity 7   Expanding a sentence

You can use *which + will + be* to expand a sentence to link your non-academic interest even more directly to university. For example:

Visiting art galleries is eye-opening and inspires me to be more adventurous in my own artwork, ***which will*** *be helpful on a Fine Art degree.*

1 **Expand one of your ideas from Activity 6 with a *which* clause. Choose from this list.**

   a   … which will be useful when I have to be self-reliant at university.

   b   … which will be an advantage when I have to be well-organised at university.

   c   … which will be a benefit when I have to get along with people of many different backgrounds at university.

2 **Write one or two interesting sentences of your own using *which + will + be*.**

3 **Complete the paragraph with the correct form of the words in brackets.**

Rock climbing with a mountaineering group is my main leisure interest. Climbing is (challenge) and (use) a wide range of skills. It has (equip) me with many survival skills and (teach) me how to solve problems under pressure. It has also helped me (assessment) risks, be (responsibility) and (building) close friendships. The activity is very (exhilarate) and a good way to make new friends, which will be a great advantage when I start university. I am a more (confidence) and (organise) person as a result of my rock-climbing experience.

Activity 8   Writing about your leisure interests

1 Now use your notes to write at least one paragraph describing your leisure interests. Before you start writing, plan what you are going to write using this list.

Remember to:

- say what you are interested in and what activities you enjoy
- explain what makes the interests and activities so enjoyable
- emphasise how much you gain from them
- say how they will benefit you at university
- add any other interesting ideas of your own
- avoid starting all sentences with 'I' – use a variety of openings.

2 After you have written your first draft check it to make sure you have highlighted the benefits of your leisure interests. Make any improvements and write your final draft.

3 Proofread your final draft and correct any errors. If you can, show your final draft to one or two friends and ask for their feedback. Do you agree that their ideas better reflect the 'real' you? If necessary, write a last version, incorporating any changes.

Activity 9   Positions of responsibility

Positions of responsibility are excellent for your personal statement because they show that you are capable and resourceful. This could include helping in a school or community organisation, event or facility, running a club, being a prefect or team captain, or any work experience, paid or voluntary.

1 Think carefully about any positions of responsibility you have had. Brainstorm some ideas on paper (rough notes are fine). Keep all your ideas as you will find them very useful later.

This is what Jared wrote:

> Supervising the school swimming pool has helped me mature and has given me insight into how exercise can benefit people of all levels of ability. This experience has given me practical insights which will be helpful in my sports degree.

2 Write full sentences using these words.

a cooking/my family a few times a week/improved my skills and knowledge/will/helpful/I have to manage/a small budget/university

b work in/call centre one evening/week/confident talking to people/useful/speak in seminars/ university

c repair electrical goods/shop/methodical/advantage/engineering degree/university

d work/assistant/music studio/summer holidays/teach/me/independence/how/manage/my time/ under pressure/useful/when/have busy schedule/university

Activity 10   Writing complete paragraphs

1 **Now use your notes to draft at least one complete paragraph about any positions of responsibility you have held. Before you start writing, plan what you are going to write using the list.**

Remember to:

- explain briefly what you do or have done
- explain how this experience will definitely benefit you at university
- add any other interesting ideas of your own
- avoid starting all sentences with 'I' – use a variety of openings.

2 **After you have written your first draft check it to make sure you have highlighted the benefits appropriately. Make any improvements and write your final draft.**

3 **Proofread your final draft and correct any errors. If you can, show your final draft to one or two friends and ask for their feedback. If necessary, write a last version, incorporating any changes.**

Activity 11   A model application

 Ivan is applying to study a degree in architecture. Architects plan and design buildings. What skills do you think would be helpful for this? What practical examples might Ivan provide to show that he has these skills, or the potential to acquire them?

1 **Read Ivan's personal statement.**

I am applying to university to do architecture because it is a fascinating subject that *integrates* academic studies with practical applications for modern life. In addition, the subject will give me the chance to develop my imagination and my *aesthetic sense* and to learn a wide range of technical and vocational skills.

I have been interested in architecture since I was about ten, when a new extension was built at my school. Seeing the work carried out was very *intriguing* and I was amazed at how our *cramped* building was transformed into a spacious place.

What I find especially interesting about the subject is how architects have to balance beauty with practicality. My subject reading mirrors this interest and I have read widely around the topic. I particularly admire the work of Ali Samona on the Arabic heritage and, from a completely different *perspective,* Karl Marsson who has written extensively about contemporary Scandinavian style. Both architects have challenged the *boundaries* of modern architecture in *innovative* ways.

In the sixth form, I have most enjoyed art, design and maths. Membership of The Artists' Club and the Mathematicians' Society has enabled me to experiment creatively with more imaginative ideas and new concepts. For example, feedback from my peers inspired me to be more adventurous in my art project 'Personal Space'. In addition, the practice I had at the Mathematicians' Society motivated me to use more complex equations in my eco-living study.

Where work experience is concerned, I volunteer at a play scheme for young children with disabilities one afternoon a week. I also deliver early morning newspapers at weekends. Through this work I have become more *empathetic* and methodical which will be useful on my university course.

In terms of leisure interests, I find sketching, especially sketching *urban* scenes, *fulfilling* and it has improved my observational skills. My sporting activities include playing for my town football team and we won last year's regional cup final. As well as keeping me fit, the game is a great way of relieving pressure in intensive periods of study at college.

Studying at an English-speaking university is my first choice because of the world-class teaching reputation and facilities. Although I am not a native English speaker, I have been taught in English since I was 13, and I passed my IGCSE ESL with grade B two years ago. I have continued to perfect my knowledge of English and I am sure I will manage well in an English-speaking environment.

Regarding my future career, I may want to become an architect working in private practice or for a local authority in town planning. Whatever I choose, I know that if I continue to be conscientious, hard-working and eager to learn, my degree will open many doors for me.

2 **Read these sentences about Ivan's personal statement and answer Yes or No.**

a He gives sensible reasons for applying for architecture.

b He provides a relevant practical example to illustrate how he first became interested in buildings.

c He shows evidence of wider reading and explains what he has gained from it.

d He discusses the relevance of clubs he belongs to.

e He explains the benefits of his work experience.

f He links his leisure interests to his application.

g He justifies his decision to study at an English-speaking university.

h He shows knowledge of future careers in architecture.

i He divides his text into appropriate paragraphs and starts with good introductory phrases.

j He has a good standard of vocabulary, sentence structure, punctuation and spelling.

k Overall, he sounds enthusiastic and committed to his chosen goal.

3 **Find words in italics in Ivan's personal statement which are similar in meaning to these words.**

a with little space or room

b awareness of what is beautiful

c deeply satisfying

d associated with a city or town

e combines

f able to understand the feelings of others

g limits

h way of thinking about something

i using new or inventive methods and ideas

j very curious and interested in something

Activity 12 Achieving an enthusiastic tone

Sounding positive and enthusiastic in a personal statement is important.

1 **Read Ivan's personal statement again and underline any verbs, nouns, adjectives or other expressions which sound positive and enthusiastic e.g. admire, fascinating.**

2 **All the adjectives in the box on the next page describe positive personal qualities, except one. Decide which one is the odd word and write down an opposite, positive word instead.**

empathetic	versatile	resourceful	conscientious
selfish	eager	resilient	methodical
adventurous			

3 **Complete these sentences using words from the box above. There is one more word in the box than you need to complete the sentences.**

a Satwinder approached analysing the data in a very _____ way, and underlined any surprising or unusual findings.

b Doctor Mangat was known for being understanding and _____ , not only about the suffering of the sick patient but also about how illness affected the whole family.

c The manager knew he could trust Chinua not to make careless errors with the accounts and thought of him as one of his most reliable and _____ members of staff.

d Our team captain is a _____ person and recovered quickly from the shock and disappointment of not winning the competition.

e Although Oliver had enjoyed studying the theory of banking, he was _____ to increase his knowledge through a real job in a bank.

f Alice was a _____ cook and adapted all kinds of dishes from many cultures for her restaurant menu.

g I love being _____ and hope to sail round the world before I am 30.

h Fahima could not afford to buy expensive materials for her project but she was able to create a wonderful, original project through recycling old discarded items. Her unusual and _____ approach won her a special award.

4 **Read the adjectives in the box. Decide which adjective cannot be used to describe a person.**

focused	determined	committed	successful
spacious	talented	persevering	imaginative
energetic	efficient	independent	confident
calm	dedicated	analytical	

5 **Tick any of the adjectives that reflect your attitudes and skills. Then choose one or two and use them in a sentence about yourself.**

Activity 13   Ways to avoid starting with 'I'

There are several other easy ways to avoid starting a sentence with 'I'. For example:

I have been taught in English since I was 13, although I am not a native English speaker.

can be reorganised as:

Although I am not a native English speaker, I have been taught in English since I was 13.

Consider the following sentences. How could you reorganise them so they do not start with 'I'? Remember you sometimes need a comma after the introductory clause.

1 I visited and read aloud to elderly residents in a retirement home between 2010 and 2011.

2 I have been chairperson of the Entrepreneurs' Club since January of this year.

3 I won a prize for my still-life painting in an art competition sponsored by local businesses.

4 I travelled to Sri Lanka with the school choir after I was chosen to be the principal soloist.

5 I was asked to demonstrate basketball techniques to younger pupils as I have a achieved a high standard in the sport.

6 I achieved a national newspaper award for 'Most Innovative Physics Project' when I was 16.

Activity 14   Clubs and societies

1 Clubs and societies can include college clubs, town or village clubs or membership of relevant online groups. In his personal statement, Ivan referred to his membership of relevant clubs. Which clubs do you belong to? How do you think your membership has helped get you closer to your goals?

Make notes about any clubs or society you belong to and what you have gained from them in relation to your university application.

2 Ivan's football team won the cup final. Have you ever achieved any particular awards, certificates, prizes or any special distinctions? Have you ever entered any competitions? Even if you do not win, this shows enthusiasm and commitment.

Make notes about any prizes or awards you have won.

Activity 15   Using the correct punctuation

Add the correct punctuation and capital letters to this paragraph about membership of a club.

i have been an enthusiastic member of the student business club since starting my pre-university course the club aims to increase members knowledge through discussion of business news in both the electronic and print media our debates have helped me tremendously in researching my recent economics project on globalisation which involved selecting material from a wide range of information sources in addition twice a term local business people are invited to give us talks on topics including marketing investment and dealing with business challenges finally the insights i have gained from the speakers practical experience have inspired me to choose international business for my degree

Activity 16   Choosing the best word

Choose the correct word from the pairs of words in italics.

I always thought I would do maths at university *because/after* I had enjoyed maths at school and wanted to study the subject in more detail. *However/Surely*, when I got to university, I found university maths very different from my previous studies where I had worked on set methods. Finding different ways to solve maths problems began to defeat me and I felt out of my *weight/depth*. *Nevertheless/Moreover*, there was little choice about the modules I could take which was frustrating.

After careful *thought/worry*, I decided to leave the course and got a job in a chemist's shop dispensing medicines. Pharmacy began to feel more and more exciting and, after work, I looked *up/out* topics on the Internet and discovered fascinating research papers on various websites.

Eventually/Shortly, I reapplied to university to do a degree in pharmacy which has been just right. *It/There* is a broadly-based course, combining theory and hands-on work. Career options are very attractive *too/to*, and include opportunities in a wide range of settings.

Activity 17   Writing a complete personal statement

You now have all you need to prepare an effective personal statement which reveals all that is best about your qualities, skills and attainments. You will enjoy this final activity because you will now see clearly for yourself how much you have achieved in your life.

Your personal statement will provide the evidence the university needs to see that you will be successful on your chosen course and you are worthy of being offered a place.

Now write a complete personal statement that includes all the aspects you have covered in this part of the unit.

PART 2 WRITING A CV AND COVERING LETTER

CV stands for *curriculum vitae*. This is a Latin term and it means the 'course of life'. In practical terms, your CV is a brief outline of your education, skills and experience.

A CV is often required by employers because it shows them, at a glance, whether you are a suitable applicant. It can also be used when you apply for voluntary work.

Hints and tips for writing a good CV

- Be brief and to the point — a single page is ideal.
- Present information in small sections.
- Use appropriate headings, sub-headings and bullet points.
- Give your *most recent* educational and work experience first (work experience can include voluntary work).
- Pay extremely careful attention to grammar, punctuation and spelling.
- Keep a copy of every CV you send out.
- Keep your CV up to date.
- Use good quality paper and envelopes if you are sending your CV by post.

Activity 18   Analysing a CV

Ahmed wants to work in the sports and leisure industry. Read Ahmed's CV.

Name: Ahmed Roshan
Address: 16 Saray El Gezira Street
Zamalek 11211
Cairo
Egypt
Mobile: 07718293610
E-mail: ahmedr@newmail.co.com
Age: 18

Personal profile
I am a motivated, hard-working individual, eager to achieve the first step in the sports and leisure industry. Currently, I am looking for a challenging part-time position while completing my studies. Ideally, I would like a position that offers the opportunity to learn from more experienced colleagues and work my way up.

Main achievements
- Team captain for school rugby.
- Achieved a National Sports Academy Activity Leader for Children Certificate in my own time last year, enabling me to work with children in holiday clubs.
- Raised considerable funds for my local hospitals through fun runs.
- Attained a high standard of personal fitness, training regularly at my local gym.
- Organised a desert camping trip for friends and myself last year.

Education
Cairo Academy 2009–2011
York School 1998–2009

IB Predicted grade 2010 – 34 points overall

IGCSE	Physical Education	A*
IGCSE	Maths	A*
IGCSE	English Literature	B
IGCSE	English Language	B
IGCSE	History	C
IGCSE	Geography	B
IGCSE	Science	B
IGCSE	Applied Science	C
IGCSE	Food Technology	B
IGCSE	ICT	C
IGCSE	French	A

Work experience

Play leader – voluntary position, June–August 2009

As a play leader, I was responsible for organising children's activities at Heliopolis Holiday Centre. I devised the sports programmes, taking into account the children's ages and any special needs. The work improved my ability to plan, my communication skills and confidence.

Hobbies and leisure interests

My hobbies include keeping fit, swimming and all team sports. I also support my city basketball team and often watch them play. Languages are a particular passion of mine and I have recently begun teaching myself Spanish through a home-study course.

Additional information

Learning to drive

Referees

Mrs M. Baxtam
Headteacher
Cairo Academy
PO Box 340
Cairo
Mobile: 3901267
E-mail: baxtamm@gmail.com

Mr Al-Nomeini
Head Sports Coach
Heliopolis Holiday Centre
New Road
PO Box 3241
El Morrreya-Heliopolis
Cairo
Egypt
Tel: 02 22670087

Read these statements about Ahmed's CV and answer Yes or No.

a   He includes his personal details.

b   He provides an outline of his profile, goals and key attainments.

c   His most recent experience is given first.

d   He gives details of suitable referees.

e   He gives information in short sections, with sub-headings and bullet points.

f   He has kept his CV short.

g   There are no errors in spelling, punctuation, grammar or vocabulary.

h   Overall, Ahmed has highlighted aspects of his experience which are relevant for the sports and leisure industry.

Activity 19   Writing your own CV

1   Write your own CV, using the structure below and the example in Activity 18 as a guide.

- Personal details
- Personal profile
- Key achievements/skills
- Education
- Work experience/positions of responsibility
- Hobbies and interests
- Additional information (optional)
- Referees

2   Draft and redraft your CV until you are completely satisfied with it.

Proofread it carefully. Ask a friend to check it as well if you can. It should not contain any errors. If possible, do this on a computer and keep a back-up copy.

Activity 20   Writing a covering letter

You usually have to write a covering letter to go with your CV.

Hints and tips for writing a covering letter

- Address your letter to a named person.
- Say that you are enclosing (or attaching with an email) your CV in support of your application.
- Say which position you wish to apply for.
- Say where and when you saw the vacancy advertised.
- Tailor your letter to the specific requirements of the job you are applying for.
- Give reasons why you think you are a suitable applicant.
- Show that you have some knowledge of your potential future employer.
- Say that you are able to attend an interview, indicating suitable times if necessary.
- Keep your letter short – no more than three main paragraphs.
- Pay close attention to grammar, punctuation and spelling.
- Keep a copy of your letter and the job advertisement.

Here is an example of a covering letter in response to a job advertisement. Read the letter and choose the best word from the pairs of words in italics.

Dear Mr Alain/Dear Sir/Madam,*

Please find enclosed my CV in support *to/of* my application for the position of Beach Hotel Catering Assistant for this year's summer season as advertised on the company website on 2 April.

I feel I am ideally *arranged/suited* to this position as I am a highly motivated, energetic person *who/that* is well organised and able to work *under/against* pressure. I also have good experience in catering, as I have helped prepare and *serve/give* food at my uncle's restaurant. As you will also see from my CV, I achieved a Food Hygiene Certificate *while/during* I carried out this work. From your company website, I was interested to *note/tell* that you attract many tour groups from Italy. I will be especially well *placed/positioned* to welcome these visitors as I can speak the language fluently.

I would welcome the opportunity to meet you at any time to discuss the position further.

Yours *sincerely/faithfully*,*

*Always use the person's name, if you know it. If you use their name, finish the letter 'Yours sincerely'. If you don't know their name, use 'Dear Sir or Madam' and finish with 'Yours faithfully'.

Activity 21 Applying for a job vacancy

1 This job vacancy appeared on the website rightjobplease.com on 1 May. Read the advertisement carefully and underline any important parts. Then think about the skills, experience and personal qualities that an applicant might mention in a covering letter.

Bright Futures

YOUTH-WORK ASSISTANT

Bright Futures is a new project which aims to help young people achieve their potential. We require a youth-work assistant to help run an activity club for young people aged 12–14 on Thursday evenings from 6pm to 9.30pm. The club, which is located in the city centre, offers teenagers the opportunity to socialise in a friendly atmosphere and learn some basic skills. Applicants should have the ability to help with at least two of the following: sports, photography, IT, crafts, music. Applicants need to be friendly and imaginative and have an interest in helping teenagers. Experience desirable but not essential as training will be given.

Send your CV with covering letter to:

Mr Brendan Elmore
Bright Futures
Linton Grove
Wellstead
Dublin 1
Ireland

---

2 You decide to apply for the vacancy. Write a covering letter using the outline below.

Your address

The date

Recipient's name and address

Dear _____,

Please find enclosed my CV in support of my application for _____.

I feel I am a suitable applicant for this position because _____.

I would love to discuss this position further and am available for interview _____.

Yours _____

Activity 22   Proofreading

Here are some sentences from covering letters. There is a mistake in each sentence. Find the mistake and correct it.

1   It would be a pleasure to work on such an innovative company.

2   As you will see from my CV, I have passed qualifications in advanced mathematics.

3   I am an energetic and sociable person and eager helping elderly people.

4   Work experience in an insurance company enabled me to gain myself confidence.

5   The company where I worked was quite small so I was often required to make decisions by my own.

6   I noticed that your company recently received a national award for the high quality of it's products.

7   While working in a repair shop, I acquired a good knowledge for a range of electronic equipment.

8   Last year, I spend three months completing a course in hospitality.

9   I am available for interview any day accept Wednesday, as I attend a first-aid course on that day.

10   I look forward too meeting you and explaining how my experience is relevant to your organisation.

Activity 23   Academic style – avoiding slang

Slang and colloquialisms should be avoided in both academic writing and when applying for work. Replace the words in italics with more formal words.

1   Training to be a *kids'* dance instructor is challenging work.

2   According to reports in the *papers,* the company has recently expanded into the soft drinks market.

3   The supervisor told me I had done a *cool* job.

4   Hard work has never *bothered* me.

5   He has been *into* computers since primary school.

6   I believe in law and order and plan to become a *cop* when I leave college.

7   Working as a junior assistant in a TV studio might seem glamorous, but in reality the job is *not up to much.*

8   I visited the university on an open day to *check it out* for myself.

9   Taking care of the children involved looking after their clothes and other *stuff.*

Activity 24   Responding to a job advertisement

1 This vacancy was advertised in *The Daily Post* on 2 June. What does the job involve?

Be Perfect

SATURDAY CUSTOMER SERVICE ASSISTANT/RECEPTIONIST

Be Perfect manufactures male and female clothing for a range of high street stores. We require a Saturday assistant for our sales desk. Duties include dealing with customer enquiries by email and maintaining our database. You will also be required to welcome clients visiting the firm. Good interpersonal skills, a methodical approach and IT skills essential. Ability to speak another language an advantage as many of our clients are from overseas. Position would suit student who is interested in a future career in the clothing industry.

Send CV and covering letter to:
The Manager
Be Perfect Ltd
22 Bankhill Road
London SE1 4VW

2 You decide you would like to apply for this position. Read the advertisement again very carefully, underlining any important elements you should mention in your covering letter.

3 Write a rough draft of the covering letter that will accompany your CV.

4 Proofread it very carefully, asking a friend to check it as well, if possible.

5 Write further drafts of the letter, until you are satisfied that it is completely appropriate and correct.

6 Alternatively, find your own job advertisement advertising a vacancy that appeals to you and write the covering letter.

Activity 25   Spelling

In the box is a list of words commonly used when applying for jobs. Many of them have appeared in the unit so far. Use the 'look, say, cover, write' technique you learned in Unit 2 to help you memorise them.

candidate	applicant	advertisement
vacancy	supervisor	qualified
qualifications	completing	opportunity
position	energetic	enthusiastic
responsible	motivated	methodical
conscientious	committed	efficient
imaginative	friendly	sociable
experience/experienced	sincerely	faithfully
attached	enclosed	suitable/suitability
available/availability	convenient/convenience	company
manufacturer	skills	abilities
certificates		

Activity 26   Analysing a job application

Michelle is a university graduate hoping to improve her career prospects. She wishes to apply for the following position.

Read both the job vacancy and Michelle's CV carefully, highlighting any experience she has that is relevant to the job.

Eco-Holidays Business Co-ordinator

Eco-Holidays is a rapidly expanding tourism company offering environmentally friendly holidays. We require a skilled business co-ordinator with good people skills for our sales office. You will be responsible for increasing business and managing a small dynamic sales team. Tourism or business experience essential.

Email your CV and covering letter to:

Mr David Lee
Managing Director
Eco-Holidays
1290 New Manton
Hong Kong
Email: dlee@ecoholidays.com

Michelle Dupont

Address: Flat 8, 57 Rose Avenue, Victoria Park, Domester, MX3 5QW
Tel: 07796242669 **Email:** mdupont@student.domester.ac.uk

Personal profile

I am a highly motivated and dedicated person with a strong academic background and excellent analytical skills. I have varied experience in business sectors and am seeking a career in Tourism or Business Development.

Key skills

- Good interpersonal skills. Worked as a volunteer at a day centre for adults with learning difficulties during student vacations.
- Leadership and problem-solving skills. Led a group of teenagers on a wilderness holiday experience last summer. Rapidly promoted to Team Leader in most recent employment.
- Bilingual in French and English. Learning Chinese.

Education

2006–2009   University of Domester, Scotland
BSc Economics (2.1), modules completed in:
- Business Analysis, Mathematics, General Economic Theory, Economic Development

1999–2005   Raleigh International School, Paris
- 3 AICE levels: Maths (A), French Literature (A), Physics (A)
- 10 IGCSEs: 5 A*, 3A, 2C

Experience

2009–2010   **Dream Holidays Ltd**   **PROJECT ASSISTANT**

- Part of a small sales team managing and renting out short and long term holiday apartments. Promoted to Team Leader.
- Devised an Advanced Rental Programme which simplified the business process and increased company profits.
- Designed a company website promoting a professional brand image and helping to stimulate company growth.

May–Sept 2008   **Eagle IT**   **REPAIR SCHEDULE ALLOCATOR**

- Organised repair schedules for computer engineers. Co-ordinated several schedules simultaneously, maximising engineers' efficiency.
- Directed engineers over the phone, developed good interpersonal skills.

Additional Information

- I raise funds for Ecology International, a charity that exists to protect rare plants.

Interests

I am an enthusiastic tennis player and also run competitively. I enjoy foreign travel, dancing, socialising and reading science fiction novels.

References

Suleiman Mohammad
Managing Director
Dream Holidays Ltd
15 Parkway
Glasgow Gl2 7BJ

Activity 27   Further practice

1 Imagine you are Michelle and write a covering email to accompany her CV when she applies for the job. Invent any extra details that would strengthen her application. Draft, redraft and proofread the covering letter until you are sure it is right.

2 For further practice, collect examples of real job vacancies that are suitable for you. Then practise your skills by applying for them with a covering letter and a CV.

Answer key

If there is no right or wrong answer to a question, we have not provided an answer in this key. For suggested answers to the longer writing tasks, please see the Model answers section on page 144.

UNIT 1 WRITING EVALUATIVE REPORTS

Activity 1

1 1c; 2d; 3h; 4e; 5a; 6g; 7f; 8j; 9b; 10i

Activity 2

participants; clip; eyewitnesses; generalised; ethical; differentiated; cross section of society

Activity 3

1   Alex wanted to find out whether language has an influence on memory.

2   The participants were shown film clips of traffic accidents and were asked to estimate the speed of the vehicles, using questionnaires.

3   His hypothesis was proven.

4   The strong points were that the wording of the questionnaires was effective and differentiated well between emotive and non-emotive language. He also analysed the data accurately and his results were reliable. The weak points were that the participants were not eyewitnesses to real road accidents so his results could not be generalised. Moreover, the sample was not big enough.

Activity 4

1   You may include the view that people tend to respond to emotive language. Doctors and dentists may use calming, non-emotive language when discussing health problems with patients, to minimise upsetting them. Becoming objective about your work is a skill which improves with practice, enables you to be more independent and self-reliant, and means you can take constructive criticism from others less personally.

2   Alex's report has a title, a clear aim, is clearly organised with headings and numbered points, only contains relevant information, has a reasonably formal style, includes suitable vocabulary, and has correct spelling, punctuation and grammar.

Activity 5

1   b Precise measurements were taken. c Small groups were tested. d The participants were told about the aims of the investigation. e Valid results were obtained. f The apparatus was set up correctly. g The participants were taken into a separate room. h Conclusions were drawn from the data. i The results were generalised. j The validity of the observations was checked.

2   The passive constructions in the report are:

Thirty participants were selected for the investigation which was carried out …

Participants were shown six film clips …

When participants were given ....

... my results could not be generalised.

Activity 6

1 • The park was the right environment for the observation. If I do this investigation in future, I will use a similar playground environment because it helps children feel at ease.

   • The individual interviews were too time-consuming. They took one hour per child. If I do a similar investigation again, I will interview children in pairs.

2 • In the experiment, the stopwatch broke down. If I do this experiment again, I will have spare equipment available.

   • The temperature of the liquids was measured at 30 minute intervals. This was too infrequent. If I repeat this experiment, I will measure the temperature every ten minutes.

   • The sodium chlorate ran out halfway through the experiment. If I do this experiment again, I will check the stock levels in advance.

   • The observers were using different methods so there are no reliable conclusions. If I do a similar investigation in future, I will make sure all observers are trained in the same methods.

Activity 7

1 traffic accident; 2 high-crime area; 3 adverse circumstances; 4 risky; 5 criminal; 6 inform; 7 enemy; 8 an unbelievable account; 9 crowd; 10 talking

Activity 8

There are no right or wrong answers to the questions at the beginning of the activity, but research shows that women are more collaborative workers than men and are more likely to discuss ideas, reassure each other and work with others to achieve a shared outcome, whereas men tend to prefer to work on their own.

1 1 Aim

    2 Hypothesis

    3 Procedure

    4 Findings

    5 Conclusions

    6 Evaluation

        Strengths

        Weaknesses

2 1 Aim: My objective was to investigate the behaviour differences between male and female students in the library.

    2 Hypothesis: I believed that females would be more likely to work together, whereas males would work alone.

    3 Procedure: I spent six hours using a specially devised behaviour checklist to observe male and female behaviour in the university library on 10 May. The checklist included a way of recording male and female behaviour during my observations. The checklist and data breakdown are available in the appendix.

    4 Findings: It was found that females were twice as likely as males to work in pairs or small groups.

    5 Conclusions: Females are more likely than males to actively seek out peer group support while studying.

    6 Evaluation

Strengths

I carried out a valid investigation and the results matched the hypothesis.

Weaknesses

As I was working alone, I was only able to observe a small area of the library. If I do another observation, I will work with a group of observers so that we can observe interaction in the Learning Resources room and Multimedia Suite.

Activity 9

2 The equipment was contaminated, so it was destroyed. 3 The records were confidential, so access was denied. 4 The statistics were out of date, so these were not used. 5 The solution was reheated during the experiment, so the results cannot be guaranteed. 6 Many participants left the trials early, so conclusions could not be drawn. 7 Needle stick injuries are/were common among medical students, so additional training is/was required.

Activity 10

1 take in; 2 run out of; 3 looked into; 4 broke down; 5 set up; 6 put away; 7 put forward; 8 went through; 9 put on; 10 took up; 11 gave up; 12 put up

Activity 12

Corrections are in bold. Errors are crossed out.

Procedure

- Twenty male students were **recruited**. All volunteers ~~there~~ followed a calorie-controlled diet for six weeks. They ~~made~~ **did** 45 minutes of daily exercise.
- The volunteers ~~they~~ were weighed and measured weekly.
- At the end of the programme, half the volunteers (Group A) ~~resuming~~ **resumed** a normal eating pattern. They were also ~~on~~ asked to do 45 minutes of exercise every day. The remaining volunteers (Group B) returned to their usual eating pattern but were ~~them~~ not given special instructions about exercise.
- ~~Since~~ **After** three months, volunteers in Groups A and B were weighed and measured again.

Findings

- At the end of the six-week programme, the volunteers ~~who~~ had lost between 4 and 6 kilos. They had reduced waist measurements ~~buy~~ **by** up to seven centimetres.
- After three months, none of the volunteers in Group A had put on ~~their~~ weight. All the volunteers ~~which~~ in Group B had regained up to three kilos.

Conclusion

- Following a daily ~~Exercise~~ **exercise** programme of 45 minutes per day will help maintain weight loss.

Evaluation

Strengths

The feedback received from the volunteers showed that they:

- had been highly motivated ~~to~~ **on** the programme
- would be ~~when~~ willing to take part in further research.

Weaknesses

- The timescale for the follow-up period ~~it~~ was limited to three months. I felt this was ~~to~~ **too** short. I will use a ~~more~~ longer timescale in future.
- The sample ~~were~~ **was** not representative enough. In future, I will recruit volunteers ~~coming~~ from a wider cross section.

Activity 13

1 containers; 2 rodents; 3 shapes; 4 insects; amphibians; 5 synopsis; 6 bush; habitat; 7 discrepancies; 8 defendant; 9 withdrawal symptoms; cravings

Activity 14

See Model answers.

Activity 16

1 cinematography – technical aspects of making a film

peers – people of a similar age or in a similar situation

voice-overs – voice of an unseen commentator heard during a film or play, etc.

2 The correct answer to questions 1 to 10 is Yes. It is a good report.

Activity 17

1 Qualitative evidence is more suitable because Elena is eliciting the views and opinions of her peers, in order to find out their personal responses to the film.

2 Your answer may include the idea that if Elena works out in more detail the end result, she will be able to plan better and be clearer about how she could achieve her desired outcome.

Activity 18

1 a memorable; b allocated; c insufficient; d edit; e peers; f voice-over; g discarded; h objectively

2 a peers; b edited; c allocated; d objectively; e memorable

Activity 19

b My first idea was to base my musical composition on a folk song, but this was too simplistic, so we used a Bach chorale.

c Originally a forest location was chosen, but the light was not bright enough, so we used a coastal area.

d My first idea was to make the costumes in velvet and silk, but this was too expensive, so I used cotton and wool.

e My first idea was to set the story in Warsaw, but this needed too much research, so I chose an area familiar to me.

f Originally the aim was to explore the effect of war on a family, but this was too wide-ranging, so I focused on the effect on one main character.

g My first idea was to paint a still life of apples on the kitchen table, but this was too mundane, so I painted apple trees in an orchard.

h My first idea was to use slow, romantic music in the opening scene, but this was too sad, so I chose a lively, more upbeat soundtrack.

Activity 20

2

Strengths

1 outcomes; 2 permission; 3 targets; 4 setting; 5 safely

Weaknesses

1 scheduled; 2 prosthetic; 3 adapt; 4 intrusive

Future plans

- advice
- subjects

Summing up

- deprived
- self-esteem
- atmospheric
- feedback

Activity 21

See Model answers.

UNIT 2 WRITING REPORTS ON SURVEYS

Activity 1

There are no right or wrong answers to the questions at the beginning of the activity, but responses could include ideas such as the possibility that the public may feel nervous and unsure of what to expect if they volunteer for research, especially if they lack experience of work of this kind. Ways scientists can allay fears could include giving full information beforehand and explaining any risks.

1 The aim of the report is to summarise how effective the volunteers found the fitness tests, and the reasons why people volunteered for the research.
2 A questionnaire was used for collecting data.
3 The information in the report is clear.
4 The statistics are easy to understand.
5 The report is well set out.
6 The study was ethical and fair.

Activity 2

1 asked for – elicited; people who complete a questionnaire – respondents; separate part of the report – appendix; exercise machine – treadmill

2 a elderly; personal; b side effects; trial; c useful; habits; d number; clinical; e appendix; f fee; fares; g vomit; h prescription; tube

Activity 3

- Just under all – 99.7%
- Over one in ten –10.8%
- Half – 50.0%

- Almost half – 49.2%
- Nearly two-fifths – 39.7%
- An insignificant proportion – 0.03%
- More than one in six – 17.3%
- Just over two-thirds – 66.8%
- Nearly a quarter – 23.9%

Activity 4

1 **A substantial proportion** is more appropriate.

2 Figures released yesterday show that young people are failing to lead active lives. Only **just over two-thirds of children** aged 7–12 take sufficient daily exercise to maintain health. The figure falls in the teenage years with **just under half** of teenagers doing enough daily exercise. For those between 20 and 30 the figure falls to **about one quarter**. There are fears that a sedentary lifestyle may lead to health problems. Health organisations predict that obesity rates may rise by **a third** over the next twenty years. A health promotion campaign starting on major TV channels aims to increase the popularity of exercise and will emphasise the importance of a balanced diet.

Activity 5

1 **Active constructions (examples):**

In May, 94 participants completed a questionnaire.

Finally, they gave their views on participating in scientific research.

Passive constructions (examples):

Height, weight and body composition were measured by the scan.

Respondents were asked to say whether their main reason for taking part in the study was to support research or get information about their fitness.

2 a It is proposed that the number of participants in the study is/should be increased to 60.
   b It is recommended that volunteers should be told/are told about any physical abnormalities we detect.
   c It is proposed that the benefits to the participants of knowing their fitness levels are/should be emphasised.
   d It is recommended that volunteers should rest after the exercises.
   e It is proposed that volunteers are told not to/should be told not to smoke before the tests.
   f It is proposed that the heart rates of volunteers are measured.
   g It is recommended that participants should be told/are told they can withdraw at any time the tests are being conducted.
   h Finally, it is recommended that volunteers under the age of 18 are not recruited/should not be recruited.

Activity 6

1 The problem was that 400 out of 500 of those surveyed said they would not take part in research. This information is being used by the research team to improve the way they recruit volunteers and carry out trials.

2 a Most respondents were worried they would feel uncomfortable being interviewed or examined by the research team.
   b The research team could ask volunteers to visit the hospital to meet staff informally, make sure clear information leaflets are available, put information on the website for volunteers, and offer telephone support and contact.

Activity 8

1 Participants walked continuously for twenty minutes on the treadmill.

2 Any volunteers under the age of 18 were not allowed to participate unless they had a signed parental consent form.

3 All information is confidential and any information identifying individuals is removed from the documentation.

4 A final recommendation is that volunteers are invited to the laboratory before the start of the study, so that they can become familiar with the scientific environment.

5 A period of relaxation and rest was enjoyed by all the participants at the end of the laboratory tests.

6 Some volunteers developed a minor and localised skin irritation from wearing the heart monitors, but this went away on its own.

Activity 9

1 pick up; 2 switched off; 3 fell through; 4 took back; 5 dropped off; 6 see through; 7 carried out; 8 worn off; 9 cut back; 10 taking part; 11 measured out

Activity 10

See Model answers.

Activity 12

1 minor; abnormal; public; major; popular; obese
2 Possible examples:

- Cost was only a **minor** feature in the planning and organisation of this project.
- Unfortunately, the baby was born with an **abnormal** kidney which had to be corrected by surgery.
- The King's former palace is now a **public** building and used for exhibitions and musical concerts.
- The opinions of the customers were naturally a **major** concern in our survey of the shopping centre.
- Sardinia is a **popular** place for holidays and hotels are often fully booked in the summer season.
- Josephine is not **obese**, she is only a little overweight.

Activity 13

2 The answer to questions a, e, f, g and h is Yes. The answer to questions b, c and d is No. It is a good questionnaire.

Activity 14

2 The more precise questions are 1B and 2A.

Activity 15

1 The question more likely to influence the respondent is 1B.
2 Possible answer:

1 Tick the answer which best reflects your views.

a People in general are less interested in tennis than they used to be.

b People in general are more interested in tennis than they used to be.

c I am not aware of a change in people's interest in tennis recently.

2 Where do you play tennis most frequently?

    a   a tennis club?

    b   a sports centre?

    c   at school/college?

    d   another place?

    If your answer is d, please specify where you play tennis most frequently.

3 In a typical month, how many times do you play tennis?

    a   Once or twice

    b   Three to five times

    c   Six to eight times

    d   More than nine times

4 In the future, do you plan to:

    a   Play about the same amount of tennis as you do now?

    b   Play less tennis than you do now?

    c   Play more tennis than you do now?

Activity 16

See Model answers.

UNIT 3 WRITING A FOR-AND-AGAINST ESSAY

Activity 1

1 These are the meanings:

  • heart, liver, kidneys or another major organ

  • organ donor, given with the permission of the bereaved family, or in the case of kidneys, possibly from a living person

  • someone whose own organ is failing

  • success rate is variable.

Activity 2

Key words are underlined below.

<u>Organ transplants</u> are <u>costly</u> and <u>do not always work</u>. However, <u>research</u> into, and <u>operations</u> involving, organ transplants are <u>increasing</u>. This is a <u>waste</u> of <u>time</u> and <u>money</u>.

<u>Write an essay evaluating this opinion.</u>

Activity 5

1 people claim; because; However; as

2 Finally, **the opponents of organ transplants say** that medical research is too expensive and only helps a small number of people. **They argue that** it would be better to direct funding into researching more common illnesses. **While it is true** that relatively few people ever need organ transplants, organ transplant research has brought many benefits to unrelated health issues **such as** diabetes and cancer.

Activity 6

I aim to show why I am in favour of...

Activity 7

The best conclusion is A because it answers the question and reflects what Pedro actually does in the essay.

Activity 8

1 anaesthetic; 2 anti-rejection drugs; 3 donor; 4 disfigured; 5 hormone; 6 recipient; 7 ethical; 8 arteries and veins; 9 plastic surgeon; 10 wound; 11 bereaved; 12 graft

Activity 9

Scientists are now able to experiment on animals using a transgene, which is a gene that has been altered in some way. Most transgenes are inserted into farm animals to improve their natural traits. It is claimed that transgenic techniques mean more precise and cost-effective breeding. The opponents of transgenic methods say that the technology is unethical and should not be allowed because of the terrible effects it might have.

Activity 10

1   People often want plastic surgery for cosmetic, not medical, reasons.

2   Research involving animals has resulted in successful heart surgery, joint replacements, organ transplants and drugs for cancer and diabetes.

3   If we are going to find a cure for HIV, we need to know what causes the disease.

4   All the clinical studies, with the exception of the study on diabetes, involved human volunteers.

5   To sum up, health education and improved sanitation are the best ways of avoiding disease.

Activity 11

There are no right or wrong answers to the questions at the beginning of the activity, but possible answers include the idea that people may be disturbed by the sight of a facial abnormality and react negatively to the disfigured person. Also, psychological distress may result if a person is disfigured and feels different from other people. Opportunities in employment may be reduced because of discrimination and forming relationships may be more difficult.

1   Key words are underlined below.

Facial transplants are wrong. The face has too much importance to be suitable for such an extreme form of surgery.

Write an essay evaluating this opinion.

Activity 12

1   Key words are underlined below.

Medical experiments on animals are essential if medicine is to progress. The suffering of animals used in experiments is therefore justifiable.

How far do you agree or disagree with this opinion?

2   Extra ideas to add to the list include:
   • Many cures and treatments have been developed e.g. drugs, new techniques, new anaesthetics.
   • Transgenic methods bring new hope for incurable diseases.
   • Animal experiments have been improved and refined.
   • People are very dissimilar to animals so the knowledge gained is not useable.
   • Alternative techniques are available e.g. computer modelling, robotics.
   • Transgenic methods increase the number of animals in genetic research.

Activity 13

Corrections are in bold. Errors are crossed out.

Medical experimentation on ~~animal~~ **animals** arouses many strong views. **In this essay**, I am going to show that, although animal research has led to medical advances such as the polio vaccine and heart transplants, overall it is cruel and unnecessary.

In the first ~~one~~ **place**, it is argued that medical research has led to important advances in medical understanding such as blood circulation and the role of hormones. While there may be some truth in this, we do not need ~~using~~ **to use** animals in experiments these days, as we have alternative research methods, including computer modelling and robotics.

Secondly, scientists say animals in research are cared for well and that they are ~~gave~~ **given** anaesthetics and good food. However, ordinary citizens ~~they~~ do not know for sure what goes on in laboratories. It could be that animals suffer immensely and ~~dying~~ **die** in great pain.

Furthermore, although we are told ~~us~~ that animal experiments are being improved, new developments in transgenic methods have increased the suffering of animals. A dog, for example, may be given ~~jeans~~ **genes** from a cow, which can lead to terrible effects on the dog.

To sum up, although it is true that medical experiments on animals have led to treatments and cures for some illnesses, modern developments mean ~~their~~ **there** are better alternative methods available. In my view, animal experiments should be ~~reduce~~ **reduced** and eventually stopped completely.

Yes, Brima did use this structure.

Activity 14

1 a   There is the chest clinic where heart transplants are carried out.
   b   Marisa works in a clinic which does not charge patients who cannot afford to pay.
   c   I work with a woman whose daughter is training to be a brain surgeon in Milan.
   d   October 1st is an important anniversary when we celebrate my father's recovery from surgery.
   e   Every day, I drive past the hospital where all my children were born.
   f   We never found out the name of the person who saved my brother from drowning.
   g   The nurse examined the wound which was about 10 centimetres long but not very deep.
   h   A general anaesthetic is not used on patients whose medical history makes it inappropriate.
   i   Skin grafting is a specialised technique which works particularly well in the case of burns victims.

2 a   Nurses give pain-relieving drugs to any patients who appear to be in pain.
   b   Are you going to destroy the medicines which are out of date?
   c   I wanted to help a mother whose child needed a bone marrow transplant.
   d   We carry out research to find out which people develop the disease.
   e   Is that the room where all the equipment is sterilised?
   f   Good patients do what the doctor tells them.
   g   Can you understand what those people are saying?

Activity 15

These are the expressions that should be deleted:

My granddad believes; I was watching something on TV which said; Loads of my friends think; You shouldn't always believe what you read in the papers; That problem has never bothered me; It's going to be ages before; It's a bit scary.

Activity 16

1 gene; 2 gene therapy; 3 genetic diagnosis; 4 hereditary disease

Activity 17

There are no right or wrong answers to these questions, but possible responses could include:

1   Parents might feel that it is not natural; they may have religious or moral reasons; they may be happy to accept the genetic condition as part of their life.

2   Patients must have multiple rounds of therapy to achieve any long-term benefits; viruses are often used as a carrier for new genes, but the viruses can cause other problems for the patient; there is a risk of stimulating the immune system to attack the new gene; some of the most commonly occurring genetic disorders are caused by problems in multiple genes but therapy works best on single genes.

3   People with genetic disorders could be discriminated against by employers; employers may have to cover long-term sick pay if a genetic condition occurs, so perhaps they should know about it?

Activity 18

3   The correct answer to all the questions on the approach Maryam has taken is Yes. It is a good approach.

4   The sentence which is missing from Maryam's essay belongs in the fifth paragraph, just before the final sentence.

Activity 19

1 root; 2 effects; 3 cell; 4 priceless; 5 harm; 6 intolerable; 7 Nevertheless; 8 assess; 9 advice; 10 However

Activity 20

These words should have capital letters:

Easter; New York College of Science and Engineering; Tallinn; Professor Garcia; Tuesday; Atlantic Ocean; TB; Australian Foundation for Birth Defects; November; United Nations; Chinese Centre for Technology Strategy; Alzheimer's disease; Ramadan; Marie Curie

Activity 21

3   See Model answers.

UNIT 4 WRITING PROBLEM-SOLVING ESSAYS

Activity 1

1   a   Global warming is the increase in the average world temperature.

   b   One of the main causes is pollution by carbon dioxide emissions.

   c   Possible effects include: milder winters; unpredictable weather patterns; drought; increased rainfall; flooding; melting of polar ice caps; rising sea levels; a rise in the number of mosquitoes leading to increase in malaria.

   d   Reduce fossil fuel pollution; use renewable sources of energy; recycle more, and more efficiently.

2   a renewable sources of energy; b polar ice caps; c melting; d emissions; e drought; f recycling; g fossil fuels; h threat; i pollution

Activity 2

1   Key words are underlined below:

Global warming is a serious problem. What measures could be taken by governments and individuals to control global warming and reduce its harmful effects?

4 The point which is not relevant to the topic is:

Increase budget allocation for research into space exploration.

Activity 3

1 should take action; One solution; could be reduced; could adjust; Another solution; could buy; can cut down; Reducing … recycling … would all help

2 Secondly, at a national and international level, governments should implement ways to reduce pollution. One solution is to set targets for the reduction of carbon dioxide emissions. Governments **could/can** monitor the output from power stations, for example, to ensure pollution levels are as low as possible. **An additional solution** is to develop alternative sources of energy such as wind power. **Moreover**, governments **could/can** support local people by improving public transport and recycling facilities. **Finally**, I believe governments should sign international agreements promising to cut carbon emissions.

Activity 4

1 Finding solutions to global warming is essential if we are to protect the environment. In my view, the most effective approach is for governments and individuals to work together to find solutions. In this essay, I am going to show how we can all take responsibility to protect the earth for ourselves and future generations.

2 The best conclusion is A because it sums up solutions given earlier, and it is positive and realistic.

Activity 5

1 acid rain; 2 ozone layer; 3 tidal power; 4 carbon footprint; 5 greenhouse effect; 6 wind farm; 7 green tax; 8 nuclear energy; 9 carbon sinks; 10 fossil fuels

Activity 6

1 Although wind farms have become a popular source of renewable energy, in some areas residents complain of noise vibration and disfigured landscapes.

2 As a way of reducing their carbon footprint, businesses are encouraging staff to use company buses rather than drive to work, but many employees are still reluctant to give up their own transport.

3 As well as being important carbon sinks, the rainforests are a rich source of medicinal flowers and plants.

4 Local people have prepared for climate change by building storm shelters, storing food and water supplies and increasing their insurance cover.

5 Even though the lake still looked pure and beautiful, acid rain had destroyed all the plants and insects that once lived there.

6 Companies who want to develop forest areas for business purposes will now have to pay a green tax on any profits made from business activities.

Activity 7

1 b A further solution is to move people living on the coast to homes further inland.
  c Another solution is to impose penalties if emissions from power stations are above an acceptable level.
  d An additional solution is to grow crops which require little water.
  e A further solution is to control emissions of nitrous oxide from planes and cars.

2 Possible answers:
  • A further solution is to **increase the level of street cleaning.**
  • A further solution is to support farmers to **improve methods of irrigation and fertilisation.**

Activity 8

1 b Governments **should** encourage people to protect themselves from the effects of ozone layer depletion. For example, media campaigns **could** emphasise the importance of wearing a sun hat and long sleeves.

   c Tourist agencies **ought to** ensure heritage sites and traditional cultures are not damaged by visitors. For instance, numbers visiting a particular place **can** be limited, and funds raised **could** be used to improve local people's way of life.

   d Environmental agencies **must** control coastal erosion. For example, they **could** ban excavation or building developments in sensitive areas.

2 Possible answers:

   a For example, **they could respect local customs and use local transport.**

   b For instance, **they could show people turning off the tap while they brush their teeth or suggest rainwater is collected for cleaning or watering plants.**

   c For example, **they can arrange emergency first aid and build temporary shelters.**

Activity 9

Overfishing is seriously depleting the world's stock of fish. **However**, there are ways we can protect our fish stocks and ensure a good supply of fish for future generations. **For example**, governments can set quotas to limit the amount of fish that can be taken out of the oceans. **Moreover**, fishing for certain kinds of fish which are in danger of extinction could be stopped completely. To avoid unintentional damage to fish, methods of fishing could **also** be more humane. **Finally**, governments should monitor fishing activity and penalise companies which break the rules.

Activity 10

2 See Model answers.

Activity 12

2 a Cutting the price of food **may reduce** poverty.

   b Increasing the price of tobacco **may discourage** smoking.

   c Increasing the length of prison sentences **may deter** criminal activity.

Activity 13

2 d General step a Research and monitor developments and keep relevant statistics.

   e General step k Follow official advice and change behaviour if necessary.

   f General step h Develop strategies in case there is an unexpected crisis.

   g General step f Prepare for expected changes by developing the infrastructure.

   h General step b Cooperate with other countries to find solutions.

Activity 14

See Model answers.

Activity 15

2 Key words are underlined below:

<u>Most</u> of us <u>agree</u> that it is <u>important</u> to <u>take account</u> of the <u>needs</u> of <u>older people. What</u> do you think <u>can be done</u> by <u>official agencies</u> to <u>support older people? What</u> could <u>older people</u> do to <u>help themselves</u>?

4 Relevant ideas include:

   • Allow older people to stay in their jobs if they want to.

   • Save for old age/use pension schemes.

Activity 16

1 Corrections are in bold. Errors are crossed out.

Life expectancy in many countries has been increasing steadily and my friends look forward to their grandparents attending their graduation ceremonies. An increased life expectancy raises ~~there~~ **there** many issues. In this essay, I will outline what elderly people can do to ensure ~~them~~ a good future **for themselves** and also discuss ways official agencies can give support.

In the first place, I believe older people should ~~to~~ **to** expect a tranquil and creative future. One solution to the lack of interest in life suffered by some elderly people is to have new challenges. Positive experiences such as travel will renew their energy. Older people also want to do things for others, so encouraging ~~their~~ **them** to help in charity projects ~~it~~ **it** is very rewarding.

The government can ~~playing~~ **play** a role too, in supporting older people by providing appropriate goods and services. For example, health care and public transport could ~~they~~ **they** be tailored to the needs of the elderly. Furthermore official bodies can ~~arranging~~ **arrange** financial help or provide worthwhile pension schemes.

2 In conclusion, I think that a combination of government planning, social support and personal determination will allow older people to live peacefully. They should be able to remain deeply interested in life and be free from unnecessary worries.

3 Some problems Rachel did not mention include:
- death of husband or wife
- increasing infirmity
- poverty
- medical expenses.

Activity 17

1 gather; 2 expect; 3 waist; weight; 4 depleted; 5 balanced

Activity 18

1 Key words are underlined below:

In many parts of the world <u>obesity</u> is becoming a <u>health issue</u>. <u>Children</u> in particular are <u>at risk</u> of developing <u>serious obesity-related illnesses later in life</u>.

<u>What can be done</u> by <u>governments</u> and <u>families</u> to <u>limit</u> the <u>increased incidence of obesity in children</u>?

2 See Model answers.

Activity 19

has; by; of; factors; onset; of; incidence; pace; role; for; mechanism; ensures; who; for

Activity 20

1 Key words are underlined below:

An international <u>survey</u> suggested that <u>young people lacked</u> a sense of <u>purpose</u>. The <u>report claimed</u> that <u>young people</u> were <u>less happy</u> today <u>than</u> their <u>grandparents were</u>.

<u>What</u> do you think <u>could help</u> young people <u>improve</u> their <u>motivation</u>?

2 The correct answer for each of the questions a to j is Yes. It is a good essay.

3
- different from everyone and everything else – unique
- looked for – sought
- simple, basic – humble
- problems causing delay – setbacks
- have commercial value/something people will pay for – marketable

4 Paragraph 1: Introduction
Paragraph 2: Identifying unique strengths
Paragraph 3: Parental support in achieving goals
Paragraph 4: Success comes in small stages
Paragraph 5: Summing up

5 Two examples are:
- Working for success becomes a habit.
- Goals should be planned and achieved in small stages.

6 The quotation means that there is always a means of achievement even if it is not quick or easy.

Activity 21

1 model; 2 rundown; unfavourable; 3 setback; 4 marketable; 5 overcame; 6 goal

Activity 22

1 Key words are underlined below:

<u>Many people</u> are still <u>too poor</u> to <u>participate</u> fully in <u>society</u>. <u>What</u> can be done to <u>reduce poverty</u> and <u>increase social opportunities</u>?

3 See Model answers.

UNIT 5 DISCUSSING ADVANTAGES AND DISADVANTAGES

Activity 1

1 Here is a possible answer:

For example, children may have their own TV sets in their bedrooms and **this means that parents cannot control what they watch on TV.**

2 Key words are underlined below:

<u>TV ownership</u> has <u>increased dramatically</u> in many parts of the world. Although <u>many people believe</u> TV has many <u>more benefits than drawbacks</u>, there are others who think <u>TV has had negative effects</u> on our lives.

<u>Discuss</u> the <u>advantages and disadvantages</u> of the <u>increase in TV ownership</u>.

Activity 3

Secondly; also; Finally; Nevertheless; drawbacks; As a result; A further concern is that; for instance; If; In fact

Activity 4

The correct introduction is A as it reflects more clearly the main points of the essay.

Activity 5

1 a   To sum up, the advantages of nuclear power outweigh the disadvantages, **but only if safety checks are carried out regularly.**

   b   To conclude, the expansion of the home entertainment industry outweighs the drawbacks, **as long as we have censorship to protect morals and values.**

   c   The disadvantages of being self-employed outweigh the advantages **because it is a more risky and insecure way of earning a living.**

   d   The disadvantages of English becoming a world language are greater than the advantages, **as local languages will suffer and people will lose interest in learning them.**

2 A possible way to complete the sentence is:

To sum up, I think the advantages of going abroad to study outweigh the disadvantages, **provided that students are well prepared for the experience**.

3 A possible way to complete the sentence is:

In conclusion, I think the disadvantages of teenage marriage outweigh the advantages, **because young people may be unable to finish their education if they are married**.

Activity 6

1 more careful; more understanding; stronger; closer

2 A family visit to the ballet is **more memorable than** watching a DVD at home and may be a talking point in conversation between parents and children for many years.

3 Watching sports events on TV is not **as thrilling as** being a spectator at the actual event because you cannot share the tension of the crowd in the same way.

4 Attendance at theatres is falling as a result of the increase in home entertainment. As a result, tickets have become **more expensive than** they used to be.

5 Society is becoming **more passive** as a result of the expansion in home entertainment and people are **less enthusiastic** about going out to see a play or concert.

6 People used to be **more aware** of the physical and emotional efforts made by live performers.

Activity 7

In the first place, students find the courses inspirational and gain a wonderful opportunity to develop themselves as creative artists. **For example,** they learn how to evaluate arguments and to think independently. When they graduate, there is a wide range of careers open to them. **Moreover,** there is 'artistic' work in their specialisms and careers in the media, advertising and marketing. **Finally,** even though the job market is competitive, many graduates find good employment and are extremely successful.

Activity 8

1 Key words are underlined below:

<u>Advertising techniques</u> have become <u>more sophisticated</u>. There are <u>many</u> who <u>think</u> this <u>change is a positive development</u>, <u>but others</u> have expressed <u>concern</u> about the possible <u>negative impact</u>. <u>Explore the benefits and drawbacks of advertising for the consumer</u>.

3 Encourages people to spend too much and get into debt.

Activity 9

1 Corrections are in bold. Errors are crossed out.

Advertising is now so pervasive that it is difficult to ignore it, whatever part of the ~~word~~ **world** you live in. Advertising has had some positive ~~affects~~ **effects** but it also has negative implications for people. In this essay, I am going to consider the influences of advertising ~~to~~ **on** the consumer.

Advertising undoubtedly has many ~~advantage~~ **advantages** for the consumer. It helps consumers to be more aware of the products that are available and ~~there~~ **their** particular qualities. People are, therefore, in a better position to make decisions about what to buy and how much to spend, which is especially helpful if you live in a ~~Rural~~ **rural** area. For example, I live 50 miles from a town and find it more convenient to check the products advertised on the Internet to make sure they are what I ~~wanting~~ **want**, than to travel all the way to the shops only to be disappointed.

Nevertheless, there ~~is~~ **are** a number of drawbacks to advertising. The most serious problem is that advertising ~~prays~~ **preys** on people's fears and insecurities. For example, some advertising techniques aim to persuade us that a hair gel will ~~it~~ make us more popular and successful. Even very ~~much~~ confident people are vulnerable to this kind of influence. In fact, advertising techniques can be so subtle that we may be unconscious ~~off~~ **of** their influence.

To ~~summing~~ **sum** up, I believe that the disadvantages of advertising outweigh the advantages because some adverts exploit people's insecurities. People ~~which~~ **who** are lonely or sad will not feel more positive just because they have bought a shampoo. Advertisers ~~they~~ encourage false wants based on insecurity. As the product does not ~~meat~~ **meet** a true need, it cannot satisfy the real requirements of the consumer.

2 The sentence that was removed belongs in the third paragraph after the first sentence. There are no right or wrong answers to the second part of this question.

Activity 10

The corrected verb forms are in bold:

Up until about 100 years ago, advertising was unsophisticated and was mainly **focused** on providing information about products. People's shopping habits **were** rational. People would not, for example, buy a new coat until their old coat had **worn** out. However, revolutionary psychological research **changed** this attitude. The research **demonstrated** that people were **driven** by their needs for respect, love and a sense of emotional worth. Sales people were **trained** to make the connection between people's need to feel good and shopping. So customers were made, in subtle ways, to feel less important or less respected if they did not **buy** expensive products. At the same time, clever advertising techniques **reinforced** the message that buying prestigious goods **made** you more important. Advertising **became** a thriving industry which was further **helped** by growing prosperity and the introduction of the credit card.

Activity 11

2 See Model answers.

Activity 12

1 pervasive; 2 values; 3 made; 4 exploit; vulnerability; 5 imagery; 6 subtle; 7 self-conscious; 8 preyed; 9 aspire

Activity 14

1 customers; 2 Swimmers; 3 Tourists; 4 patients; 5 Players; 6 Students

Activity 15

2 Neuroscientists say every experience leaves a **mark** on the human brain. The effect of high levels of computer usage on the brain is unknown, but there are fears that it could affect our emotional development, be **habit-forming** and lead to shortened **attention** spans. These effects are greatly increased by the expansion of computer use during our leisure time. Children, whose brains are still developing, are at most risk from high levels of usage. Perhaps because of parental fears about the safety of playing outdoors, the amount of time a child spends playing **computer** games or chatting on online sites has **doubled** in the last three years. This has particular implications for children because they do not have the life experience to compensate for the new **mindset** they may be developing. Some experts believe we may be bringing up a generation of children who fail to relate fully to others, concentrate properly or see the consequences of their **actions.**

Activity 16

1 Key words are underlined below.

<u>Social networking</u> <u>sites</u> are very <u>popular</u> in some countries. Clearly, many <u>people enjoy talking to friends on the sites</u>, but <u>experts warn</u> that social networking <u>sites</u> could be <u>harmful</u>.

<u>Compare and contrast the benefits and drawbacks of social networking sites for individuals</u>.

2 All the statements 1 to 9 are true. It is a good essay.

3 There are no right or wrong answers to this question.

4 signals–cues; relating–interaction; comfort–reassurance; exciting–stimulating; ability–capacity

5 The sentence belongs in the second paragraph after the fifth sentence.

Activity 17

The ideas Prakash chose not to include are:

- can be addictive
- thoughts and feelings posted instantly, without reflection – reduces inhibitions/sense of what is private
- conversations can be time-wasting
- rapid interchange – constant stimulation
- instant feedback.

Activity 18

1 empathy

2 instant gratification

3 inhibition

4 body language

5 online imagined societies

6 identity

7 mindset

Activity 19

1 The key words in the essay question, including those saying what to do, are underlined below:

Many places which were once small towns have become big cities. This change may be slow or relatively fast. Explore the advantages and disadvantages of urban development.

6 See Model answers.

UNIT 6 WRITING OPINION ESSAYS

Activity 1

The final sentence of the paragraph should be completed with option B as follows:

As a result of the survey, a leading scientific institute decided to **create a public website showing the aims of projects and their progress**.

Activity 2

1 Key words are underlined below:

The media sometimes report that expensive scientific research has been a waste of money. What are your opinions of the research work scientists do? Are the benefits worth the expense?

3 The sentence should be added to the Drawbacks column.

Activity 3

1 The correct introduction is A because it reflects what Ayesha actually does in her answer and also stays on the topic set in the question.

2 As I see it; For instance; but; Furthermore; For instance; In my view; so

3 should; fail; worthwhile; benefits; twice

There are no right or wrong answers to the questions at the end of the activity, but possible responses could include:

- the idea that scientists can refuse to carry out work they think is not ethical
- the idea that public understanding of scientific work and scientists themselves might improve with more media involvement directed towards making their work accessible to the general public.

Activity 4

1 The words used to introduce reasons are **because** or **as.** The words used to introduce opinions are **In my view, As I see it** and **I believe.**

The examples could be written out in full like this:

    a   For example, recent newspaper reports claimed that scientists had found the gene to stop ageing, which was a distortion of the truth.
    b   For instance, some scientists continue with research even if there is a possibility the projects could do harm.
    c   For example, students might not find a job if they do not understand scientific principles.
    d   For instance, scientists believed stomach ulcers were caused by stress, but further research showed that bacteria caused them.
    e   For example, research into rare medical conditions uses money and skills that could be better used for researching common diseases.
    f   For instance, cancer research costs a great deal of money but has led to much higher survival rates.
    g   For example, rich countries have been criticised for unethical research done in poor countries.

2 The sentences could be completed like this:

    a   It is very limited to judge students' success on academic performance alone, **because not all intelligent students are good at exams**. For example, **many students who do badly in exams, do very well at practical tasks**.
    b   As I see it, it is unwise to condemn all scientists **because they cannot control the way their discoveries are used**. For example, **when Einstein was developing his revolutionary new theories, he did not think nuclear weapons would be developed as a result**.

Activity 5

1 exaggerated; 2 stereotypes; 3 inevitable; 4 trial and error; 5 break even

Activity 6

1 faultless
2 genius

Activity 7

1   Scientists' autonomy is very important to them.

2   Is a physicist's work just a job, or is it a vocation?

3   Engineers say that their work produces many benefits for the nation's economy.

4   Even geniuses acknowledge their team's efforts. As the famous scientist Newton said, 'If I have seen a little further, it is by standing on the shoulders of giants.'

5   The project was presented at a conference for ministers. The ministers' first reaction when the project's leader, Professor Kelly, explained the outcomes of the research, was one of unanimous disbelief.

6   The universities' research staff spoke at a TV journalists' convention to explain their latest breakthrough.

7 He was working as the research assistants' administrator and frequently attended meetings on their behalf.

8 The photographs were stored on several CDs.

9 The government has asked its ministers to review the privacy laws.

Activity 8

2 Key words are underlined below:

<u>Experts</u> sometimes <u>leave their home country</u> to take up <u>new jobs abroad</u>. Recent <u>media reports</u> suggested that this <u>trend is likely to increase</u> further. <u>What are your opinions on this issue</u>?

3 See Model answers.

Activity 9

1 There are no right or wrong answers to the question. Possible answers include:

They make life more interesting/relaxing/entertaining. They give us beautiful/unusual things and help us see life in a new way.

2 Key words are underlined below:

Many <u>creative people</u> producing artistic work are <u>poorly paid</u> and find it <u>difficult to live</u> on their <u>earnings</u>. Is this <u>situation acceptable</u>? <u>What are your opinions</u>?

Activity 10

1 The extra words are crossed out and in bold.

The media portrayal of creative people often gives the impression that **these** they are usually wealthy people. While it may be true that a few artists are rich, many do not make **there** a decent living, even though they are talented and produce original work. In this essay, I shall suggest some strategies to improve **well** the income of creative people.

In the first place, the public **we** could be educated more effectively about the value of an artist's work. If more people understood the effort that artists put into their work and the skills **what** they use, they would realise why they should pay reasonable prices. It may also deter people from buying illegal copies or downloading **the** music illegally.

A further solution is to encourage artists to join **with** professional associations. These associations can advise them how to market their work and what they should **to** charge for it. One of my favourite musicians, Sammy Worviel, was **he** almost cheated when he made his first record because he lacked business experience. Last but not least, artists could also **be** network with each other to build up commercial knowledge and social contacts.

2 In conclusion, the good contribution creative people make to our lives means that they deserve a fair rate of pay. I believe both the general public and official organisations could do more to protect artists from exploitation. Finally, artists themselves need to learn better ways to produce and sell their work at rates that reflect its value.

Activity 11

I have studied a range of characters portrayed in both the film and TV dramas and **I have** concluded that **they are** often depicted in a stereotyped way. Although stereotyping gives us characters who are instantly recognisable, on the whole I believe **it is** detrimental to the audience identification with the character. When teenagers are stereotyped as 'lazy' or 'rebellious', the audience **will not** feel sympathetic to them or try to understand their motives. If **we are** to relate meaningfully to the characters, they should be more fully developed. Subtle, conflicting or complex elements of their personalities **should not** be ignored or oversimplified. I think actors should challenge the director's control, if they feel **they are** asked to play a role inappropriately.

Activity 13

1 Key words are underlined below. You should answer by exploring your own opinions on the question.

TV quiz shows are a very popular and traditional form of entertainment. What do you think is the lasting attraction of the TV quiz show for the audience?

3 All the statements are true. It is a good essay.

4 Words similar in meaning are:

- being in a difficult situation in life – predicament
- a simple seat – stool
- exploited/being taken advantage of – manipulated
- something exciting we want very much though we might not get it – tantalising
- feelings of stupidity or shame – humiliation
- type of programme/artistic work – genre
- something that will last a long time – enduring
- weakness – vulnerability

5 a You can give any reasonable response. It is highly likely that audience identification and suspense are major attractions of quiz shows.
  b You can give any reasonable answer. The universal aspects include the imbalance between the powerful and the powerless, shown by the contrast between the powerful presenter and the vulnerable contestant.
  c You can give any reasonable answer.

6 a The focus of Kulwinder's essay is exploring his own opinions on the question.
  b Persuasive devices used include: identifying himself with the reader (e.g. 'we experience the thrill…'); using some short, categorical sentences (to suggest he is stating a fact); using evocative language such as 'breathlessly watching' (to create a powerful image in the reader's mind).
  c The effect of the omissions is to strengthen his argument and make it more persuasive, as it inhibits the reader from challenging his viewpoint.

7 Brainstormed points not included in Kulwinder's essay are:

- prizes often extremely large
- presenter may take role of severe judge – viewers enjoy seeing others humiliated
- lots of humour/jokes
- suspense – commercial breaks have delaying effects
- camera shots – close-ups increase suspense by showing strain on faces of contestants
- audience admires contestants' exceptional and expert knowledge.

Activity 14

1 universal
2 preserved his mystique
3 identified
4 aspire
5 worshipped
6 genre
7 glorifies
8 public image
9 publicity
10 represented
11 enduring

Activity 15

1 There are no right or wrong answers to this question. Possible reasons why some talented people do not become stars include:

They do not seem special enough or have enough talent. There is a lack of audience identification. The timing is wrong for this type of music/acting/appearance or it does not fit in with the dominant culture/does not catch the public imagination.

2 There are no right answers to the brainstorm. It is helpful to focus on one or two famous stars.

3 Key words are underlined below:

<u>What</u> is the <u>appeal of the 'star'</u> for the <u>audience</u>? Is it <u>possible</u> for a <u>'star'</u> to be <u>made overnight</u>? <u>What are your views</u>?

The second part of the question is asking for your opinions of stardom in general.

6 See Model answers.

Activity 16

1 Key words are underlined below:

<u>In your opinion</u>, how may a <u>newspaper</u> <u>influence</u> its <u>readership</u>?

3 In; a; tone; into; is; affect; coverage; appeal; serious; interviews; On the other hand; ordinary; that; of; under

6 See Model answers.

UNIT 7 DESCRIBING VISUAL INFORMATION

Activity 1

1 a Figure 4; b Figure 2; c Figure 1; d Figure 5; e Figure 3

2 Figure 1 downward trend

Figure 2 downward trend

Figure 3 upward trend

Figure 4 upward trend

Figure 5 shows no change after the initial fall.

Activity 2

2 a $600,000; b 2001; c $625,000; d 2003–06; e Harry's Bikes

3 shows; sharply; peaked; steeply; little change; gradual; significantly

Activity 3

1 a number sold; b February; c May; d 27,000; e June; f Fresh Start

2 The graph **illustrates** the volume sales of toiletries between January and August. There was a gradual **decline** in Fresh Start sales between January and April. After this however, sales rose **steeply** and 65,000 products were sold in May. Between May and June, there was little **change** in sales, but there was a gradual improvement between July and August.

In **contrast,** sales of Energise rose significantly between January and February **peaking** at 125,000 **followed** by a steep fall and period of **fluctuation.** Between July and August, fewer than 65,000 products were sold each month. Overall, the trend for sales of Energise is **down.**

Activity 4

Here is a possible answer:

Sales for Grow'n'learn did not change between January and June, staying level at $2m. Between June and December, sales rose significantly, peaking at $5m in December. In contrast, Funtime made a good start to the year as $4.3m was earned between January and March. This was followed by a steep decline however, with earnings falling to $2.5m between April and June. Sales continued with little change between June and December. Finally, PlayMe sales increased steeply between January and June, and reached a peak of $4.4m. However, sales fell sharply to $1.8m between July and September. There was a gradual increase from September, with sales reaching $2.8m in December.

Activity 5

1   1 A Birds; 2 E Plants; 3 B Reptiles; 4 C Mammals; 5 F Invertebrates; 6 D Fish; 7 G Amphibians

2   Possible answers:

Plants: rose bush; oak tree

Reptiles: lizards, crocodiles

Mammals: whale; elephants

Invertebrates: worms, flies

Fish: shark; trout

Amphibians: frog, toad

3   Possible ideas include: overfishing, hunting, poaching, trade in endangered species, climate change, pollution, loss of habitat due to farming/industrial development.

Activity 6

1   a   The degree to which the different groups are threatened with extinction.
        b   The percentage of each group threatened.
        c   Plants are the most threatened group; birds are the least threatened group.
        d   Mammals and reptiles; invertebrates and fish.

2   Figure 9 shows that **about half** of the world's plant species are threatened, making them the most endangered group in the world. **Nearly a third** of the world's fish and invertebrate species are at risk and **about a quarter** of the planet's mammal species. More than **one in five** of the planet's amphibian species are in danger. Birds are the least threatened group but, even so, more than **ten per cent** of this group are at risk.

Activity 7

1   a 1900–2000; b No; c dramatic; d smallest: mountain gorilla; largest: blue whale; e Yes

2   **According** to Table 1, only 650 giant pandas were alive in 2000 **compared** with 65,000 in 1900. The numbers of the blue whale also **fell** dramatically from 335,000 to 4,500. The **population** of the black rhino decreased **significantly** from 1,000,000 to 2,000. Finally, the mountain gorilla was also **near** to extinction, as **only** 500 were left alive in 2000.

Activity 8

1   a   southern white rhino, Natal, South Africa; golden tamarin monkey, Atlantic Coastal Forest, Brazil; elephant, Kruger National Park, South Africa.
        b   southern white rhino – over 30 years; golden tamarin monkey – over 40 years; elephant – six years.
        c   The golden tamarin monkey has increased most significantly.
        d   Possible answers include: national and international conservation programmes; animal sanctuaries/protected areas; stiffer penalties and more control of poaching and the illegal trade in animal parts; animal breeding programmes.

e   Possible answer: In 1989, elephants in Kruger National Park numbered 7,468. By 1995, this number had increased to 8,371.

2   tables; depict; diminishing; thriving; habitats; extinct; handful; turn; notable; from; has increased; presence; poachers; In addition; risen; a combination; Finally; captive; assumed; habitat

Activity 9

1   a   True
    b   False. Forest areas make up 4% of the total land area.
    c   False. Wetlands, areas of water and urban areas make up 0.7% of the total.
    d   False. Croplands are the next biggest area after shrubland and grassland.
    e   True
    f   True

2   **According to** Figure 10, over half of the total land area is shrubland and grassland. Croplands are the next **largest** area and make up 38% of the total. Areas designated as sparse and barren form 2.8% of the total area. Wetlands and land for urban use are **much less** significant and constitute less than 1% of the **total** land area. Shrubland and grassland is clearly **the most dominant feature** and **comprises** more of the total land area than all the other types of land put together.

3   Here is a possible answer (to be third sentence of completed paragraph): Forest areas, at 4%, constitute a small but significant part of the entire land area.

Activity 10

1   a forest; b shrubland; c cropland; d savannah and 'other'

2   Here is a possible answer:

According to Figure 11, forest area comprises a quarter of the land use/habitat in Asia, followed by shrubland which accounts for one fifth of total land use. Cropland is the third most significant area and constitutes over 15% of land use. Barren and sparse vegetation and grassland together make up almost one quarter of land use/habitat. Cropland and vegetation mix comprise 8.4% of land use. Savannah and 'other' are the least dominant areas and comprise 8% of the total land area.

3   As we can see from Figure 10, over half of South Africa is shrubland and grassland. This is a vital habitat for many rare species but these areas are gradually being **eroded** by sprawling **suburbs,** factories and farming. Consequently, the habitat for insects, birds and mammals is under pressure; for example, giraffes eat the **thorny** plants that grow in these grassy habitats so they are moving further afield in search of food.

In Asia, forested areas, as depicted in Figure 11, account for a quarter of the total land area. Today, the forest areas of Asia, both tropical and **temperate**, are being cleared. One of the most **poignant** examples of the effects of forest clearance is the **reduction** in the number of orang-utans which live among the palm trees of the Indonesian rainforest. Soap, food and **candles** are all valuable products of the palm trees. About 1.8 million hectares of rainforest, which includes many palm trees, are being destroyed every year for commercial reasons. **As a result** of habitat destruction, the number of orang-utans has **fallen** from 230,000 to only 60,000 in **recent** years.

Activity 11

1   a   Hectares of productive land or sea needed to resource the lifestyle of one person.
    b   The ecological footprint of each individual in selected areas of the world.
    c   The numbers of hectares.
    d   Only selected areas.
    e   The USA and the UK.
    f   India.
    g   Yes.

2   Figure 12 **illustrates** the hectares of land or sea required to resource the lifestyle of one inhabitant from selected countries. It is clear from the chart that people in richer and more

developed areas of the world consume **far more** resources than those in less developed countries. The USA is **by far the biggest** consumer of resources per head of population. For example, an individual in the USA uses almost ten hectares whereas an individual in India does not consume **even one** hectare. China **consumes only** 1.6 hectares per head of population – **under** six times less than the USA. At 5.6 hectares per person, the UK is the **next largest** consumer of resources shown on the chart after the USA.

3 Here are some possible sentences:

Brazil's footprint is more than twice as big as India's footprint.

The UK's footprint is about three times the size of China's footprint.

Activity 12

1 a The bars in Figure 13 compare the carbon dioxide emissions from a number of selected countries from the burning of oil, natural gas and coal.
 b Tonnes of carbon dioxide per person.
 c Japan and the UK.
 d No, as only information from selected countries in the world is given.

2 Figure 13 compares the **yearly** emissions of carbon dioxide from a selection of countries. There is clearly a **great** difference in levels of emissions between richer and **less developed** countries. Of the **eight** countries depicted on the chart, the largest producer of CO_2 **by far** is the USA which produces 20 tonnes per person of carbon dioxide emissions each year. This is **more than double** the amount produced by the UK or Japan.

3 Here are some possible sentences:

Senegal produces less than one tonne of carbon dioxide per year which is less than any other country shown on the chart.

India is the next smallest producer of carbon dioxide after Senegal.

Japan, Russia and the UK produce similar levels of carbon dioxide emissions.

Activity 13

1 Here are some possible answers to questions based on Figures 14 and 15.
 a Job and promotion opportunities; better educational facilities; a more exciting and diverse lifestyle; to make new friends and social contacts; more shops and social facilities.
 b Decent housing and jobs; good health care; transport networks; schools; street cleaning; sewage disposal; emergency services (police, fire service, ambulance etc).
 c By working hard; contributing to their neighbourhood; cooperating with the legal obligations of living in a city. Newcomers can bring with them energy, a range of skills, personal determination, flexibility; interesting life experiences.
 d Discussion could include the tendency for urbanisation to become more intense in poorer parts of the world. This may be because rural areas in richer countries are better serviced and provide better opportunities than some rural areas in poor countries.

2 Figure 14
 a False. The rural population was more than twice as big as the urban population.
 b True
 c True
 d False. The rural population began to level out but the urban population increased dramatically.
 e False. By 2030, the gap will be widening.

Figure 15
 a True
 b False. The urban population of Africa will increase more.
 c False. The urban population of North America will have a larger increase.

Here is a possible answer, summarising the trends in Figures 14 and 15:

According to Figure 14, global urbanisation is expected to have increased dramatically by 2030. The graph shows that there was a gradual rise in the urban population from the 1950s until 1990. After 1990, there was a steep increase in urbanisation which is projected to continue and the urban population is expected to reach 5,000 billion by 2030. The rural population is projected to level off at around 3,100 billion in 2015. Consequently, it is predicted that the world's urban population will eventually greatly exceed the number of people living in the rural areas.

Figure 15 illustrates the predicted percentage increases in urbanisation in different parts of the world. Although all areas will experience some degree of urbanisation between 2000 and 2015, it is clear that Europe will probably have the smallest growth at approximately 3%. Oceania and North America are projected to have the next smallest increases at about 16% and 20% respectively. Latin America and the Caribbean, Asia and Africa are projected to have the largest rises in urban population. Of these three areas, Africa stands out as likely to have the largest increase by far. The chart indicates that Africa is projected to experience a growth in urban population of over 70%.

3 Paragraph 1

steadily; exceeded; trend; marked; predicted; impact; affected; rise

Paragraph 2

squalor; levels; who; optimism; newcomers; named; has; exist; vibrant

UNIT 8 WRITING PERSONAL STATEMENTS AND CVS

Activity 1
3 The inappropriate reason is b.

Activity 2
1 a I am applying for this subject **because** I love analysing character and motivation.
   b I want to do this degree **as** I can arrange the course to suit my particular academic interests.
   c I am interested in this subject **because** it offers the opportunity to integrate my fascination with science with my desire to help people.
   d I am applying for this degree as it gives me the opportunity to develop critical thinking and analysis skills.

2 a Furthermore, the second term allows me to focus on one topic area.
   b In addition, I will get practical experience in a clinical setting.
   c Moreover, there is a multilingual and varied academic programme.
   d Furthermore, I can develop fluency in a European language.

Activity 3
1 a I have been fascinated by banking since the sixth form.
   b I have been curious about this subject for several years.
   c I have been enthusiastic about this subject since I did a work placement in a clinic.
   d I have been improving my knowledge of international relations for nine months.
   e I have been researching the political and cultural influences on Malaysia since last summer.
   f I have been practising my language skills for two years.

3 a–v; b–iii; c–vi; d–iv; e–i; f–ii

4 I have been fascinated by space science since I was given a telescope for my seventh birthday.

Activity 4

2 She has read three other novels by Jane Austen and two biographies.

3 a Since starting my pre-university course, I have been learning about the impact of industrial change on society. In addition to the prescribed course reading, I have been downloading business articles from the Internet. From my reading, I have learned more about the way companies respond to changes in the market.

b For the last two years, I have been interested in the work of Polanski. In addition to studying his films in class, I have been researching articles about Polanski on the Internet. Recently, I have been reading critiques of his work in journals such as *Contemporary European Cinema*. From my reading, I have learned more about the influence of Polish history on Polanski's work.

5 The correct word or phrase from each pair is in bold:

I **have been** interested in Oriental Studies **since** I was 13 **when** we had an exchange teacher from Japan at our school **for** one year. She **taught** us to speak Japanese and **introduced** us to novels by Japanese authors. I particularly like the novels by An Kazuki and can read them in Japanese with the help of a dictionary. The novels are set in the past and show how historical events **have shaped** modern Japan and made the country what it is today. **In addition**, I listen to a Japanese news broadcast each day which has developed my knowledge of vocabulary and key political figures in contemporary Japan.

Activity 6

2 a Visiting art galleries is eye-opening and inspires me to be more adventurous in my own artwork.

b Watching foreign films has given me insights into other countries.

c Making my own clothes is creative and cheap.

Activity 7

3 Rock climbing with a mountaineering group is my main leisure interest. Climbing is **challenging** and **uses** a wide range of skills. It has **equipped** me with many survival skills and has **taught** me how to solve problems under pressure. It has also helped me **assess** risks, be **responsible** and **build** close friendships. The activity is very **exhilarating** and a good way to make new friends, which will be a great advantage when I start university. I am a more **confident** and **organised** person as a result of my rock-climbing experience.

Activity 9

2 a Cooking for my family a few times a week has improved my skills and knowledge. This experience will be helpful when I have to manage on a small budget at university. (*OR . . .* which will be helpful when I have to manage on a small budget at university.)

b Working in a call centre one evening a week has helped me to be confident talking to people. This experience will be useful when I have to speak in seminars at university. (*OR . . .* which will be useful when I have to speak in seminars at university.)

c Repairing electrical goods in a shop has made me more methodical. This experience will be an advantage on my engineering degree at university. (*OR . . .* which will be an advantage on my engineering degree at university.)

d Working as an assistant in a music studio in the summer holidays has taught me independence and how to manage my time under pressure. This experience will be useful when I have a busy schedule at university. (*OR . . .* which will be useful when I have a busy schedule at university.)

Activity 11

2 The answer to each of the statements a to k is Yes. It is a good personal statement.

3 a cramped; b aesthetic sense; c fulfilling; d urban; e integrates; f empathetic; g boundaries; h perspective; i innovative; j intriguing

Activity 12

1 Other words and expressions which sound positive and enthusiastic in the context include: wide range; intriguing; transformed; especially interesting; read widely; challenged the boundaries; most enjoyed; experiment creatively; imaginative ideas; adventurous; fulfilling; great way; first choice; world-class; conscientious; hard-working; eager.

2 Odd word out: selfish; opposite of selfish: unselfish.

3 a methodical; b empathetic; c conscientious; d resilient; e eager; f versatile; g adventurous; h resourceful

4 The adjective that cannot describe a person is **spacious**.

Activity 13

1 Between 2010 and 2011, I visited and read aloud to elderly residents in a retirement home.

2 Since January of this year, I have been chairperson of the Entrepreneurs' Club.

3 In an art competition sponsored by local businesses, I won a prize for my still-life painting.

4 After I was chosen to be the principal soloist, I travelled to Sri Lanka with the school choir.

5 As I have achieved a high standard in the sport, I was asked to demonstrate basketball techniques to younger pupils.

6 When I was 16, I achieved a national newspaper award for the 'Most Innovative Physics Project'.

Activity 15

I have been an enthusiastic member of the Student Business Club since starting my pre-university course. The club aims to increase members' knowledge through discussion of business news in both the electronic and print media. Our debates have helped me tremendously in researching my recent Economics project on globalisation, which involved selecting material from a wide range of information sources. In addition, twice a term, local business people are invited to give us talks on topics including marketing, investment and dealing with business challenges. Finally, the insights I have gained from the speakers' practical experience has inspired me to choose International Business for my degree.

Activity 16

because; However; depth; Moreover; thought; up; Eventually; It; too

Activity 18

The answers to each of the statements a to h is Yes. Ahmed has written a good CV.

Activity 20

of; suited; who; under; serve; while; note; placed; sincerely

Activity 21

2 See Model answers.

Activity 22

The correct words or phrases are in bold.

1 It would be a pleasure to work **for** such an innovative company.

2 As you will see from my CV, I have **gained** qualifications in advanced mathematics.

3   I am an energetic and sociable person and eager **to help** elderly people.

4   Work experience in an insurance company enabled me to gain **self-**confidence.

5   The company where I worked was quite small, so I was often required to make decisions by **myself.**

6   I noticed that your company recently received an award for the high quality of **its** products.

7   While working in a repair shop, I acquired a good knowledge **of** a range of electronic equipment.

8   Last year, I **spent** three months completing a course in hospitality.

9   I am available for interview on any day **except** Wednesday, as I attend a first-aid course on that day.

10   I look forward **to** meeting you and explaining how my experience is relevant to your organisation.

Activity 23

1   children's/young teenagers'
2   newspapers
3   very good/competent
4   troubled/concerned
5   interested in/intrigued by/curious about
6   police officer
7   mundane/very routine/lacking in challenge
8   see/find out about the facilities
9   possessions/belongings

Activity 24

1   The job involves working on the sales desk dealing with customer enquiries by email, maintaining databases and welcoming clients.

5   See Model answers.

Activity 27

1   See Model answers.

Model answers

The models which follow are possible answers to selected questions from Units 1–6 and Unit 8.

UNIT 1 WRITING EVALUATIVE REPORTS

Activity 14, Scenario 1 (page 10)

Report on an investigation into students' use of shaded areas in the college grounds

Aim
The aim of the investigation was to find out whether students would use or avoid shaded areas in the college grounds. The shaded areas could be a way of reducing students' exposure to ultraviolet light.

Hypothesis
My hypothesis was that the shaded areas would be used, not avoided, by students.

Procedure
1) I obtained permission from the college Principal to arrange for temporary coverings to be erected in the main courtyard, where students enjoy relaxing during break times.
2) One covering was erected at the front of the courtyard near the science block and another was put up near the entrance to the sports centre.
3) I recorded the use students made of the shaded areas during morning break over a period of two weeks during the summer term. A full breakdown of the data is available in the appendix to this report.

Findings
The shaded areas were popular with the students. The data shows that the majority (over 70%) of students in the courtyard were using the shaded areas when observations were carried out.

Conclusion
Students will use shaded areas if these are erected on a permanent basis.

Evaluation
A Strengths
- I carried out a valid investigation, collected the data methodically and the results matched the hypothesis.

B Weaknesses
- The observations were carried out over a relatively short period of time.
- The observations were carried out at morning break times only, so comparisons cannot be made with other break times.

C Future Plans
If I do a similar investigation again, I will increase the number of observers. This would enable more observations to be carried out at different times of the day and over a longer period.

Activity 21 (page 15)

Report on the success of the Cooking Skills Project at Orchid Leaf Children's Hostel

1 Aim

The aim of the project was to teach children at Orchid Leaf Children's Hostel how to make a basic meal.

2 Method

a   First, I gained permission from the head of the hostel, Mrs Cheung, to carry out the project.

b   Next, I visited the hostel to meet the six children aged 11-13 chosen by Mrs Cheung to participate. I found out what experience of cooking they had and the kind of food they would like to prepare. I checked that the kitchen had suitable equipment available.

c   I devised a session plan and menu which were approved by Mrs Cheung. The project was carried out successfully on 14 June. All the children made a delicious lunch which included vegetable soup, a chicken casserole and a healthy dessert. The lunch was enjoyed by children and staff at the hostel.

3 Evaluation

STRENGTHS

a   I worked out clear aims and objectives, and the session was well planned and organised.

b   I coached the children effectively, and my cookery demonstrations were clear and well understood. The children were involved at all stages of the project.

c   The children acquired new skills and more understanding of nutrition. Their confidence increased.

d   The lunch was produced on time and was very tasty.

e   Feedback from the children was very positive and included comments such as 'Brilliant!', 'Can't wait to do it again!' and 'Cooking is lots of fun.'

WEAKNESSES

a   There was a shortage of chopping boards, so some children had to wait until others had finished using this equipment.

b   One child was allergic to strawberries, so he was not able to enjoy the fruit salad we made for dessert.

FUTURE PLANS

a   If I do this project in future, I will check that there is enough equipment. If necessary, I will be more flexible in planning the session, so that no child has to wait for equipment.

b   I will also find out if any children have allergies and take this into account when planning the menu.

UNIT 2 WRITING REPORTS ON SURVEYS

Activity 10 (page 22)

REPORT ON STUDENTS' VIEWS OF THE UNIVERSITY GYM

A Aim

The aim of this report is to summarise the results of the questionnaire about the gym and to make recommendations.

B Procedure

A short questionnaire was devised to find out the students' views.

• On 12 and 13 February, the receptionist asked students to complete a questionnaire when they arrived at the gym.

• 110 questionnaires were completed.

• The questionnaire and a breakdown of the data collected are available in the appendix.

C Findings

1. The staff were rated highly. The vast majority of respondents (over nine out of ten) rated them as pleasant, approachable, knowledgeable and well-trained.

(continued)

2. The fitness classes were also rated very highly, with almost all respondents agreeing that there was a wide range of classes on offer and that they helped students achieve their aims.
3. It was felt by almost nine out of ten respondents that the gym provided a good range of equipment.
4. In other respects, however, the gym equipment was rated poorly, with almost half of respondents not agreeing that the equipment was modern or well-maintained.
5. The cleanliness of the gym was also rated poorly, with only about one in five users agreeing that the standard of cleanliness was 'good.'
6. The showers and changing rooms were also found to be poor. Only about 15% of respondents agreed that these facilities were 'good'.
7. Only two-fifths of respondents felt that, overall, the gym provided good value for money.

D Conclusions
- While many aspects of the gym were found to be very good, some areas clearly need to be improved.
- In particular, the quality of the gym equipment, the cleanliness of the gym, and the showers and changing rooms require urgent attention.

E Recommendations
1. The treadmills and exercise bicycles are old and should be replaced by more up-to-date models.
2. The gym equipment should be checked daily and any necessary repairs completed within a week.
3. The showers should be retiled and the changing rooms redecorated within three months.
4. The gym should be cleaned more frequently during opening times.

Activity 16 (page 26)

Oasis Swimming Pool: Customer Satisfaction Questionnaire

1 In a typical month, how often do you use the swimming pool?
☐ 2 or more times per week
☐ Once a week
☐ A few times per month
☐ Less than once a month

2 Rate the following on a scale of 1 to 5, where 1 = very poor and 5 = very good.
☐ Helpfulness of staff
☐ Cleanliness of the swimming pool
☐ Cleanliness of the shower area
☐ Changing room facilities
☐ Overall maintenance of the pool
☐ General atmosphere of the pool
☐ Pool opening hours
☐ Café facilities

3 Tick the statement you most agree with.
☐ The pool offers good value for money.
☐ The pool offers reasonable value for money.
☐ The pool offers poor value for money.

4 Currently the pool closes at 5 p.m. If it opened in the evenings between 5 and 9, would you swim during these times?   Yes ☐   No ☐   Don't know ☐

5 Please suggest one change we could make to improve the experience of swimming at the pool.

_____

6 How likely are you to recommend the pool to a friend?
☐ Very likely
☐ Quite likely
☐ Not very likely
☐ I would not recommend the pool to a friend.

UNIT 3 WRITING A FOR-AND-AGAINST ESSAY

Activity 21, 3: question 1 (page 39)

Life would be better without mobile phones. What is your view?

Mobile phones arouse extreme reactions. There are those who cannot be parted from them, and may even own several, and those who see nothing good in them. In this essay, I will explain why I am in favour of mobile phones, despite the fact that, like all technology, they may have some minor drawbacks.

In the first place, it is claimed that mobile phones can lead to accidents, as people often use them at inappropriate times, such as when they are driving or operating machinery. This view may be valid to some extent, but mobile phones can also save lives. If someone needs to summon emergency help quickly, a mobile phone is a lifeline. In addition, mobile phone technology has assisted the police in solving serious crimes and ensuring that those who are a danger to society are put behind bars.

Secondly, opponents of mobile phones say they are intrusive. They point out that people use them without thought for the comfort of others. For example, passengers in a train compartment may talk business on their mobile phones and this may be annoying to those who would like to travel in peace and quiet. This may be true, but surely it would be more sensible for companies to restrict the use of mobile phones on public transport than to forbid their use altogether. What is needed is more considerate users, not blanket bans.

A further argument against mobile phones is that they carry health risks. These concerns have not been supported by research, however, and so far there is no evidence that mobile phones are more harmful than other kinds of technology. Nevertheless, I believe that it is sensible to limit the length of calls, in case future research detects a problem.

In conclusion, I think the benefits of mobile phones clearly outweigh any drawbacks. As long as people use them sensibly and with consideration for others, life is certainly better with them than without them. As I see it, the mobile phone is here to stay.

Activity 21, 3: question 5 (page 39)

There is nothing wrong with having cosmetic surgery to look good. Discuss.

Cosmetic surgery has become increasingly popular in many parts of the world, possibly as the result of more advanced techniques. There are many who wholeheartedly support the trend, but others who feel it is harmful and should be discouraged. In this essay, I will explore the rights and wrongs of cosmetic surgery and explain why I am against the practice.

Firstly, we are told that cosmetic surgery is an important way of increasing self-esteem because it allows people to enhance their appearance. There is some validity in this argument, but many patients do not become more self-confident as a result of cosmetic changes. Research shows that, after an initial improvement in self-worth, many patients quickly feel insecure about another part of their appearance and return for further operations to correct 'problem' areas. As I see it, cosmetic surgery only encourages people to chase an unrealistic ideal of physical perfection.

A further point made in support of cosmetic surgery is that it is a very safe form of surgery, and that procedures are being improved all the time. Although there may be some truth in this, all surgery carries some risks. Patients can still die or suffer serious complications after operations. Also, they may not be fully informed of the dangers, because strong commercial interests are involved. Finally, the surgery they undergo may not achieve the desired physical improvement. In fact, people whose operations have gone wrong can be disfigured for life.

To sum up, I have shown that cosmetic surgery is wrong for a wide range of reasons. It is unlikely to help patients with poor self-esteem, and I believe this problem would be better addressed through other means. Furthermore, there are health risks involved, and the results are not guaranteed. In my opinion, it would be better if plastic surgeons operated only on patients who have a genuine need, such as those who have been born with an abnormal appearance or have been disfigured through illness or accident.

UNIT 4 PROBLEM-SOLVING ESSAYS

Activity 10, 2 (page 46)

Rural migration

Rural migration may happen because people move to towns and cities in search of better jobs and opportunities. As a result, the countryside becomes depopulated and local facilities, such as shops, schools and clinics, have to close. If rural migration is to be reduced, the countryside needs to become an attractive and sustainable place to live. One solution is for governments to subsidise farming and provide local employment schemes, so that people can make a living locally. An additional solution is to attract teachers to rural schools, so that children can get a good education without moving to the city.

Another strategy for reducing rural migration is for the media to promote a positive image of rural life. For example, the media could portray the countryside as more peaceful, less polluted and safer than cities. This might inspire city dwellers to move to the countryside, and might also encourage businesses to relocate to rural areas. When jobs are created and the demand for goods and services grows, the local economy becomes strong and vibrant. As people begin to see a positive future in the countryside, rural migration will naturally slow down and may even stop completely.

Activity 14: question 4 (page 48)

Earthquakes, famines, hurricanes and other natural disasters cause terrible destruction. Discuss one natural disaster and explore ways to reduce its effects.

Natural disasters can have horrifying and long-lasting consequences, such as death, injury and serious damage to property and the environment. In this essay, I will explore how the destructive impact of serious floods can be limited though positive action by governments and individuals.

One solution is to manage floods efficiently, which means that governments need to have a coordinated plan of action should a crisis arise. They could also publicise the plans they have devised, in order to reassure the public. An additional solution is to educate the public about what they themselves should do in an emergency.

A further issue is that some countries lack the infrastructure to cope effectively with a crisis such as flooding. One strategy is for governments to ask international aid agencies for help. For instance, aid workers can evacuate people from dangerous areas, provide temporary shelters and food, and supply additional medical staff. Governments should negotiate carefully with such agencies to make sure assistance is targeted where it is most needed.

In my view, ordinary citizens ought to take some responsibility for helping themselves during floods. For example, they should stay informed of any developments, follow the guidelines issued by official agencies, and support more vulnerable members of their community. Furthermore, they can perhaps safeguard themselves against financial loss by having insurance which compensates them if disaster strikes.

In conclusion, major floods inevitably result in human suffering and environmental destruction. However, with practical, coordinated plans and the cooperation of the public, I believe it is possible to reduce the extent of the damage they cause.

Activity 18, 2 (page 51)

In many parts of the world obesity is becoming a health issue. Children in particular are at risk of developing serious obesity-related illnesses later in life. What can be done by governments and families to limit the increased incidence of obesity in children?

It is undoubtedly true that obesity is a major concern in many areas of the world. Children in some countries are now at risk of dying before their parents from obesity-related illnesses. In this essay, I will show that it is possible to reverse this trend.

(continued)

One solution to the problem of obesity is for the government to make the population aware of the need for a healthy diet. This can be done through media campaigns on television. Children could also be taught about nutrition at school so that they understand what the body requires in terms of fats, vitamins and proteins. Furthermore, the amount of sport offered at school can be increased. It has been shown, for example, that if children enjoy sport they are more likely to be the correct weight for their height and build.

Steps families can take themselves include involving children in planning healthy meals which the whole family will enjoy. This would show children that eating well does not mean eating tasteless food. In addition, children could accompany parents when they shop for groceries and help choose healthier versions of food they enjoy.

Research has shown that active children tend to have active parents. Parents should therefore consider increasing their own levels of exercise. For example, they could take their children swimming and have a pleasant a swim themselves, or go to the park and have fun playing ball games with them. As a result, children will develop good habits which may continue into adult life. This can have a positive effect on the next generation, too, as children grow up and become parents themselves.

To conclude, I have shown that there are several practical ways to bring childhood obesity under control. As well as government action through the media and schools, parents can make small but important changes at home which will make a healthy lifestyle attractive to children.

Activity 22, 3 (page 53)

> ### Many people are still too poor to participate fully in society. What can be done to reduce poverty and increase social opportunities?

Many people are affected by social and economic disadvantages which prevent them from being able to develop their lives or benefit from the opportunities others enjoy. However, there are a number of ways these problems can be overcome. In this essay I will show that social opportunities can be increased if official agencies and individual citizens work for positive change.

In the first place, governments can develop poor neighbourhoods by providing better housing and controlling rents so that families can afford decent homes. A further solution would be to improve schools in those areas by attracting well-qualified teachers who are committed to helping children from deprived backgrounds. Local public libraries could also be resourced effectively, which would help those who cannot afford to buy their own books or computers.

Another way to reduce poverty depends on people taking some personal responsibility for improving their own lives. Parents can encourage children's self-confidence by having high expectations of their potential. They can also help their children develop the self-discipline necessary to focus on their studies and achieve qualifications. If a child shows a special talent, such as in using a computer or in sport, this should be encouraged, as it could open the door to a better life.

Furthermore, social opportunities can be increased when the community works cooperatively to make the environment a good place to live. Organisations run by local people can play an important part in strengthening social participation. For example, local volunteers can provide interesting clubs for teenagers where they learn useful skills and positive values. A strong community spirit can be generated when people feel they matter, and are able to make a difference.

To sum up, I feel that a combination of government strategies and individual effort can lessen poverty and expand opportunities. This approach could help people participate more extensively in society and become responsible citizens. This not only benefits them; it benefits us all.

UNIT 5 DISCUSSING ADVANTAGES AND DISADVANTAGES

Activity 11, 2 (page 62)

Shopping habits

Shopping in prestigious stores has many advantages. Firstly, trained staff are on hand to select top quality items for valued customers. The assistants also treat shoppers with respect and make them feel that nothing is too much

(continued)

trouble. As there are no crowds and no haggling for bargains, the atmosphere is relaxed and unhurried. In addition, customers can take as long as they wish trying on clothes and deciding whether they want an 'investment' piece or just something which will attract the envious glances of others. Clothes with famous labels are also often ahead of fashion trends, so customers can find a unique outfit without fear that a friend will turn up wearing the same dress or suit. Last but not least, the packaging of goods is usually excellent, and customers leave carrying a beautifully-wrapped parcel or designer carrier bag.

On the other hand, there are undoubted drawbacks to luxury shopping. First and foremost, shoppers are unlikely to find great bargains or cheap offers. Moreover, if they ask for a discount, staff may make them feel poor and inferior. People may also get into debt buying exclusive merchandise on their credit cards. A further drawback is that luxury items can look out of place – in a student lifestyle, for example. To conclude, consumers might do better buying cheap versions of designer clothes in ordinary shops. These items may not be as good as the real thing, but they are certainly more affordable for those who are budget-conscious.

Activity 19, 6: question 1 (page 66)

> ### Winning the lottery would be a dream come true for many people, yet a recent survey showed that nearly half the winners reported lower levels of happiness than before the win. Write an essay exploring the advantages and disadvantages of winning the lottery.

For many people, buying a lottery ticket is an essential expense, even if they have little spare cash. In this essay, I will discuss the advantages and disadvantages of winning the lottery and explain why the drawbacks of becoming wealthy overnight are often underestimated.

Firstly, becoming rich through a lottery win brings many obvious advantages. Families can pay off any debts, for example, move to a large house with every comfort, and enjoy luxurious holidays and exciting hobbies. Secondly, with regard to work, the winner can give up his or her current job, especially if it is not stimulating or rewarding. Furthermore, lottery winners may feel a deep sense of peace and freedom, as they realise they can provide for their families financially, and need never worry about money again.

On the other hand, there are undoubtedly some drawbacks to sudden riches. Some lottery winners find buying an impressive house in an unfamiliar neighbourhood leads to social isolation. In addition, those who give up work may miss the companionship of their colleagues, and the sense of fulfilment they gained through their job. Without employment or the pressure to earn money, life can seem pointless. Moreover, things which once would have been special treats are available every day, and, as a result, lose their appeal. Perhaps saddest of all, some lottery winners find their new lifestyle separates them from their old friends and they feel lonely and cut off.

In conclusion, winning the lottery has many advantages as long as the winner can handle the new prosperity. The happiest lottery winners appear to be those who have been able to share their good fortune and make significant contributions to their favourite charities.

UNIT 6 WRITING OPINION ESSAYS

Activity 8, 3 (page 72)

> ### Experts sometimes leave their home country to take up new jobs abroad. Recent media reports suggested that this trend is likely to increase further. What are your opinions on this issue?

The brain drain is a trend that affects many countries in the world. Each year, for instance, a large number of doctors and scientists leave Europe to develop their careers in Australia, Canada and the United States. In this essay, I am going to discuss the rights and wrongs of the brain drain and why I am in favour of it.

In the first place, it is sometimes suggested by the media that experts should feel guilty about taking their skills abroad when their country needs them at home. In my view, however, experts have the right to develop their careers in the ways they think best, without negative criticism. Many professional skills and insights can be

(continued)

gained through the experience of working in another country. For example, experts may have the opportunity to do things which are not possible at home, such as meeting those considered most outstanding in their field, using state-of-the-art technology or exploring unusual aspects of their work.

Furthermore, travelling abroad can develop people on a personal level. Personal challenges can include learning a new language, exploring a different culture or overcoming prejudices and misconceptions. As a result, when the expert returns to the home country, he or she is in a better position to relate to a much wider cross section of society.

To conclude, the 'brain drain,' as I see it, is an expression over-used by the media to make experts feel selfish and guilty. Such guilt is out of place, in my opinion, because the modern world is oriented towards freedom and an international exchange of skills and experience. Many experts, in fact, return from abroad greatly enriched by the experience and with far more to offer those they serve at home.

Activity 15, 6 (page 79)

What is the appeal of the 'star' for the audience? Is it possible for a 'star' to be made overnight? What are your views?

The 'star' has a deep appeal for the public. In this essay, I will explore the attraction of film stars, and also consider whether TV talent shows can produce real stars with enduring qualities.

I believe a film star who stands the test of time appeals to the audience because he or she represents our hopes and dreams. We may not be consciously aware that we would like a more glamorous or fascinating life, but deep down perhaps we would. In addition, some famous stars come from disadvantaged backgrounds and we may feel a deep connection with that. They may have endured setbacks and humiliation before becoming well-known. This may strike a chord with us, as we perhaps know gifted people who are unrecognised – maybe even ourselves.

As I see it, real stars preserve their mystique because they know the audience needs to think of them in a special way, so it is important that we never know who they really are. If we did, we might discover that they are dull or ordinary. Our admiration could vanish instantly. In my view, this would be very sad, because genuine screen idols catch the public imagination. We need them to be the people we would love to be, having lives we can only dream about.

Furthermore, although some people become famous overnight, through a TV talent show for example, a blaze of publicity does not guarantee lasting success as a star. This may not be because the individuals lack talent; it may be because they do not appeal to the public imagination in a deep enough way. If we do not feel a special connection with the winners, the idea of these people being true stars will not take root in our minds.

In conclusion, I believe authentic stars have more than just talent; they are people who have a special aura. The public feels a strong personal identification with them, possibly at an unconscious level. In my view, a 'star' cannot be made overnight, unless that individual has the potential, not only to win public attention, but also to live and thrive in people's imaginations.

Activity 16, 6: question 5 (page 80)

Science is more advanced than ever. However, there is an increase in the numbers of people using alternative medicine that has not been proven scientifically. What are your opinions of this trend?

In some parts of the world, alternative medicine has grown in popularity. People may use it in preference to conventional treatment, even though there is often little scientific evidence to confirm its effectiveness. In this essay, I will explore the reasons for this change, and examine, in particular, the role of the media in influencing the public's view of alternative medicine.

In the first place, people turn to alternative practitioners, in my opinion, because of society's increasingly high expectations of the right to good health. The idea that a cure for an illness does not exist is rejected on the grounds that everyone should enjoy well-being. There is a strong belief that there must be effective treatment available somewhere, somehow. Consequently, it is now more socially acceptable to look for alternative

(continued)

remedies, especially for conditions that have no conventional cure. A generation ago, I believe society would have considered this a strange or risky thing to do.

Secondly, the media over-emphasises the risks of conventional medicine. For example, newspapers may print frightening reports of the side-effects of a new drug, or the unexpected death of a patient after a routine operation. Moreover, hospitals may be represented as uncaring places where the staff are too pressurised to do a competent job. As a result, people may consider alternative treatment in the hope that it is safer, and that the therapist will have a more sympathetic approach.

Furthermore, some people are afraid of going to a conventional doctor because of sensationalised reports of malpractice, even though such cases are actually quite rare. In contrast, reporting of alternative practitioners is often positive and highlights successful outcomes in individual cases. Little attention is given to the absence of scientific evidence for the particular therapy. Nor is the possible lack of qualifications of the alternative practitioner noted, or the fact that certain therapists may not have recognised bodies to regulate them.

To sum up, the upward trend in the use of alternative medicine is due to the rather unbalanced way health care is sometimes represented in the media. The trend is also influenced by stronger social expectations of excellent health for everyone, whatever their age or situation.

UNIT 8 WRITING PERSONAL STATEMENTS AND CVS

Activity 21, 2 (page 112)

123 Thornley Crescent
Riverside
Dublin 3
2 May 2011

Mr Brendan Elmore
Bright Futures
Linton Grove
Wellstead
Dublin 1

Dear Mr Elmore,

Please find enclosed my CV in support of my application for the position of youth-work assistant, which I saw advertised on the website www.rightjobplease.com on 1 May.

I feel I am a suitable candidate for this position because helping young teenagers make the most of the opportunities at Bright Futures is an exciting challenge which I would welcome. I am sociable and creative and my skills include photography, IT and playing the guitar. I would love to have the chance to coach teenagers at the club in these areas. At college, I play in the basketball team and would enjoy organising a team for your club.

I would love to discuss this position further and am available for interview any day after 3 p.m.

Yours sincerely,

Kelly O'Reilly

Kelly O'Reilly (Ms)

Activity 24, 5 (page 113)

123 Lime Tree Road
Blackheath
London SE3 9FQ
4 June 2011

The Manager
Be Perfect Ltd.
22 Bankhill Road
London SE1 4VW

Dear Sir/Madam

Please find enclosed my CV in support of my application for the position of Saturday Customer Service Assistant/ Receptionist, which I saw advertised in The Daily Post of 2nd June.

I feel I am a suitable applicant for this position because I am very sociable, have a methodical approach and am IT-literate. My IGCSE qualification in Computer Studies included managing databases, so I feel confident I could handle that aspect of the position. As well as English, I also speak Spanish fluently, which could be an advantage when welcoming your overseas clients.

In future, I hope to work in the fashion industry and am currently studying for a Fashion Diploma at college. My course involves researching fashion trends, and I would be delighted to use this experience to benefit Be Perfect in any appropriate way.

I would love to discuss this position further and am available for interview any day except Thursday, as I am responsible for helping new students at college on that day.

I look forward to hearing from you.

Yours sincerely

Franco Marquez

Franco Marquez (Mr)

Activity 27, 1 (page 115)

Dear Mr Lee

Please find attached my CV in support of my application for the position of Eco-Holidays Business Co-ordinator, as advertised in the Aberdeen Express on 12 October.

I feel I am well suited to the position as I am a dynamic, hardworking person and have relevant experience in managing a sales team and increasing business. After gaining experience as an office coordinator for Eagle IT, I spent a year working in sales for a travel company offering holiday lettings. I was quickly promoted to Team Leader.

My team regularly exceeded sales targets and I particularly enjoyed helping others improve their skills. The challenge of developing business for Eco-Holidays would be very exciting and I look forward to improving profits for your company.

I also notice your company offers environmentally-friendly holidays. As I am a keen fundraiser for the charity Ecology International, it would be my pleasure to further the conservation aims of your company.

I am available for interview at any time. I look forward to hearing from you and discussing further how I could benefit your company.

Yours sincerely

Michelle Dupont (Miss)